# Notable [illegible]
# Ninete[illegible] Century
## Great Deeds of Men and Nations and the Progress of the World

MW01674828

John Clark Ridpath

Alpha Editions

This edition published in 2022

ISBN: 9789356906037

Design and Setting By

**Alpha Editions**
www.alphaedis.com

Email - info@alphaedis.com

As per information held with us this book is in Public Domain.
This book is a reproduction of an important historical work.
Alpha Editions uses the best technology to reproduce historical work
in the same manner it was first published to preserve its original nature.
Any marks or number seen are left intentionally to preserve.

# Contents

# PREFACE

This little volume constitutes one number of the Christian Herald Library series for 1896-97. The title indicates the scope and purpose of the work. Of heavy reading the reader of to-day no doubt has a sufficiency. Of light reading, that straw-and-chaff literature that fills the air until the senses are confused with the whirlwind and dust of it, he has a sufficiency also. Of that intermediate kind of reading which is neither so heavy with erudition as to weigh us down nor so light with the flying folly of prejudice as to make us distracted with its dust, there is perhaps too little. The thoughtful and improving passage for the unoccupied half hour of him who hurries through these closing years of the century does not abound, but is rather wanting in the intellectual provision of the age.

Let this volume serve to supply, in part at least, the want for brief readings on important subjects. Herein a number of topics have been chosen from the progress of the century and made the subjects of as many brief studies that may be realized in a few minutes' reading and remembered for long. Certainly there is no attempt to make these short stories exhaustive, but only to make them hintful of larger readings and more thoughtful and patient inquiry.

The Editor is fully aware of the very large circulation and wide reading to which this little volume will soon be subjected. For this reason he has taken proper pains to make the work of such merit as may justly recommend it to the thoughtful as well as the transient and unthoughtful reader. It cannot, we think, prove to be a wholly profitless task to offer these different studies, gathered from the highways and byways of the great century, to the thousands of good and busy people into whose hands the volume will fall. To all such the Editor hopes that it may carry a measure of profit as well as a message of peace.

J.C.R.

# BRUMAIRE
# THE OVERTHROW OF THE FRENCH DIRECTORY

The eighteenth century went out with the French Directory, and the nineteenth came in with the Consulate. The coincidence of dates is not exact by a year and a month and twenty-one days. But history does not pay much attention to almanacs. In general our century arose with the French Consulate. The Consulate was the most conspicuous political fact of Europe in the year 1801; and the Consulate came in with *Brumaire.*

"Brumaire" is one of the extraordinary names invented by the French Revolutionists. The word, according to Carlyle, means *Fogarious*—that is, Fog month. In the French Republican calendar, devised by the astronomer Romme, in 1792, Brumaire began on the twenty-second day of October and ended on the twentieth day of November. It remained for Brumaire, and the eighteenth day of Brumaire, of the year VIII, to extinguish the plural executive which the French democrats had created under the name of a *Directory*, and to substitute therefor the One Man that was coming.

The Directory was a Council of Five. It was a sort of five-headed presidency; and each head was the head of a Jacobin. One of the heads was called Barras. One was called Carnot. Another was called Barthelemy. Another was Roger Ducos; another was the Abbé Sieyes. That was the greatest head of them all. The heads were much mixed, though the body was one. In such a body cross counsels were always uppermost, and there was a want of decision and force in the government.

This condition of the Executive Department led to the deplorable reverses which overtook the French armies during the absence of General Bonaparte in Egypt. Thiers says that the Directorial Republic exhibited at this time a scene of distressing confusion. He adds: "The Directory gave up guillotining; it only transported. It ceased to force people to take assignats upon pain of death; but it paid nobody. Our soldiers, without arms and without bread, were beaten instead of being victorious."

The ambition of Napoleon found in this situation a fitting opportunity. The legislative branch of the government consisted of a Senate, or Council of Ancients, and a Council of Five Hundred. The latter constituted the popular branch. Of this body Lucien Bonaparte, brother of the general, was president. Hardly had Napoleon arrived in the capital on his return from Egypt when a conspiracy was formed by him with Sieyes, Lucien and others of revolutionary disposition, to do away by a *coup* with the too democratic system, and to replace it with a stronger and more centralized order. The Council of Ancients was to be brought around by the influence of Sieyes. To Lucien Bonaparte the more difficult task was assigned of controlling and revolutionizing the Assembly. As for Napoleon, Sieyes procured for him the command of the military forces of Paris; and by another decree the sittings of the two legislative bodies were transferred to St. Cloud.

The eighteenth Brumaire of the Year VIII, corresponding to the ninth of November, 1799, was fixed as the day for the revolution. By that date soldiers to the number of 10,000 men had been collected in the gardens of the Tuileries. There they were reviewed by General Bonaparte and the leading officers of his command. He read to the soldiers the decree which had just been issued under the authority of the Council of the Ancients. This included the order for the removal of the legislative body to St. Cloud, and for his own command. He was entrusted with the execution of the order of the Council, and all of the military forces in Paris were put at his disposal. In these hours of the day there were all manner of preparation. That a conspiracy existed was manifest to everybody. That General Bonaparte was reaching for the supreme authority could hardly be doubted. His secretary thus writes of him on the morning of the great day.

"I was with him a little before seven o'clock on the morning of the eighteenth Brumaire, and, on my arrival, I found a great number of generals and officers assembled. I entered Bonaparte's chamber, and found him already up—a thing rather unusual with him. At this moment he was as calm as on the approach of a battle. In a few moments Joseph and Bernadotte arrived. I was surprised to see Bernadotte in plain clothes, and I stepped up to him and said in a low voice: 'General, everyone here except you and I is in uniform.' 'Why should I be in uniform?' said he. Bonaparte, turning quickly to him, said: 'How is this? You are not in uniform.' 'I never am on a morning when I am not on duty,' replied Bernadotte. 'You will be on duty presently,' said the general!"

To Napoleon the crisis was an epoch of fate. The first thing was to be the resignation of Sieyes, Barras and Ducos, which—coming suddenly on the appointed morning—broke up the Directory. Bonaparte then put out his hand as commander of the troops. Too late the Republicans of the Council of Five Hundred felt the earthquake swelling under their feet. Napoleon appeared at the bar of the Assembly, and attempted a rambling and incoherent justification for what was going on. A motion was made to outlaw him; but the soldiers rushed in, and the refractory members were seized and expelled. A few who were in the revolution remained, and to the number of fifty voted a decree making Sieyes, Bonaparte and Ducos provisional *Consuls*, thus conferring on them the supreme executive power of the State. By nightfall the business was accomplished, and the man of Ajaccio slept in the palace of the Tuileries. He had said to his secretary, Bourriene, on that morning, "We shall sleep to-night in the Tuileries—or in prison."

The new order was immediately made organic. There could be no question when Three Consuls were appointed and Bonaparte one of the number, which of the three would be *First* Consul. He would be that himself; the other two might be the ciphers which should make his unit 100. The new system was defined as the "Provisionary Consulate;" but this form was only transitional. The managers of the *coup* went rapidly forward to make it permanent. The Constitution of the Year III gave place quickly to the Constitution of the Year VIII, which provided for an executive government, under the name of the CONSULATE. Nominally the Consulate was to be an executive committee of three, but really an executive committee of *one*—with two associates. The three men chosen were Napoleon Bonaparte, Jean Jacques Cambaceres and Charles Francois Lebrun. On Christmas day, 1799, Napoleon was made FIRST CONSUL; and that signified the beginning of a new order, destined to endure for sixteen and a half years, and to end at Waterloo. The old century was dying and the new was ready to arise out of its ashes.

# HOW THE SON OF EQUALITY BECAME KING OF FRANCE

The French Revolution spared not anything that stood in its way. The royal houses were in its way, and they went down before the blast. Thus did the House of Bourbon, and thus did also the House of Orleans. The latter branch, however, sought by its living representatives to compromise with the storm. The Orleans princes have always had a touch of liberalism to which the members of the Bourbon branch were strangers.

At the outbreak of the Revolution, Louis Philippe Joseph, Duke of Orleans, fraternized with the popular party, threw away his princely title and named himself Philippe Egalité; that is, as we should say, Mr. *Equality* Philip. In this character he participated in the National Assembly until he fell under distrust, and in despite of his defence and protestations—in spite of the fact that he had voted for the death of his cousin the king—was seized, condemned and guillotined.

This Equality Philip left as his representative in the world a son who was twenty years old when his father was executed. The son was that Louis Philippe who, under his surname of *Roi Citoyen*, or "Citizen King," was destined after extraordinary vicissitudes to hold the sceptre of France for eighteen years. Young Louis Philippe was a soldier in the republican armies. That might well have saved him from persecution; but his princely blood could not be excused. He was by birth the Duke of Valois, and by succession the Duke of Chartres. As a boy, eight years of age, he had received for his governess the celebrated Madame de Genlis, who remained faithful to him in all his misfortunes. At eighteen he became a dragoon in the Vendome Regiment, and in 1792 he fought valiantly under Kellermann and Dumouriez at Valmy and Jemappes. Then followed the treason, or defection, of Dumouriez; but young Louis remained with the army for two years longer, when, being proscribed, he went into exile, finding refuge with other suspected officers and many refugees in Switzerland.

Thither Dumouriez himself had gone. Of the flight of young Louis, Carlyle says: "Brave young Egalité reaches Switzerland and the Genlis Cottage; with a strong crabstick in his hand, a strong heart in his body: his Princedom is now reduced to *that* Egalité the father sat playing whist, in his Palais Egalité, at Paris, on the sixth day of this same month of April, when a catchpole entered. Citoyen Egalité is wanted at the Convention Committee!" What the committee wanted with Equality Philip and what they did with him has been stated above.

Consider then that the Napoleonic era has at last set in blood. Consider that the Restoration, with the reigns of Louis XVIII. and Charles X., has gone by. Consider that the "Three Days of July," 1830, have witnessed a bloodless revolution in Paris, in which the House of Bourbon was finally overthrown and blown away. On the second of August, Charles X. gave over the hopeless struggle and abdicated in favor of his son. But the Chamber of Deputies and the people of France had now wearied of Bourbonism in *all* of its forms, and the nation was determined to have a king of its own choosing.

The Chamber set about the work of selecting a new ruler for France. At this juncture, Thiers and Mignet again asserted their strength and influence by nominating for the throne Louis Philippe, Duke of Orleans, representative of what is known as the Younger Branch of the Bourbon dynasty. The prince himself was not loath to present himself at the crisis, and to offer his services to the nation. In so doing, he was favored greatly by his character and antecedents. At the first, the Chamber voted to place him at the head of the kingdom with the title of *Lieutenant-General.* The prince accepted his election, met the Chamber of Deputies and members of the Provisional Government at the Hotel de Ville, and there solemnly pledged himself to the most liberal principles of administration. His accession to power in his military relations was hailed with great delight by the Parisians, who waved the tri-color flag before him as he came, and shouted to their heart's content.

At this stage of the revolution the representatives of the overthrown House and of the Old Royalty sought assiduously to obtain from Louis Philippe a recognition of the young Count de Chambord, under the title of Henry V. But the Duke of Orleans was too wily a politician to be caught in such a snare. He at first suppressed that part of the letter of abdication signed by Charles and Angoulême in which reference was made to the succession of the Duke of Berry's son; but a knowledge of that clause was presently disseminated in the city, and the tumult broke out anew.

Then it was that a great mob, rolling out of Paris in the direction of the Hotel Rambouillet, gave the signal of flight to Charles and those who had adhered to the toppling fortunes of his house. The Chamber of Deputies proceeded quickly to undo the despotic acts of the late king, and then elected Louis Philippe king, not of *France*, but of the *French.* The new sovereign received 219 out of 252 votes in the Deputies. His elevation to power was one of the most striking examples of personal vicissitudes which has ever been afforded by the princes and rulers of modern times.

# THE COUP D'ETAT OF 1851

With the overthrow of Louis Philippe in 1848, what is known as the Second Republic, was established in France. On the tenth of December, in that year, a president was elected in the American manner for a term of four years. To the astonishment of the whole world, the man so elected was Louis Napoleon Bonaparte, who had since the downfall of Napoleon been prisoner, exile and adventurer by turns. In the course of President Louis Napoleon's administration, matters came to such a pass between him and the National Assembly that one or the other must go to the wall.

In the early winter of 1851, a crisis came on which broke in a marvelous manner in the event called the Coup d'Etat. The President made up his mind to conquer the Assembly by force. He planned what is known in modern history by pre-eminence the stroke. He, and those whom he trusted, made their arrangements secretly, silently, that the "stroke" should fall on the night of the second of December. On that evening the President held a gay reception in the palace of the Elysee, and after his guests had retired, the scheme was perfected for immediate execution.

During the night seventy-eight of the leading members of the Opposition were seized at their own houses and taken to prison. The representatives of the people were hurried through the streets, and suddenly immured where their voices could be no longer heard. At the same time a strong force of soldiers was stationed near the Tuileries. The offices of the liberal newspapers were seized and closed, and the Government printing presses were employed all night in printing the proclamation with which the walls of the city were covered before morning. With the coming of daylight, Paris awoke and read:

1. The National Assembly is dissolved;
2. Universal suffrage is re-established;
3. The Elective Colleges are summoned to meet on December 21;
4. Paris is in a state of siege.

By the side of this proclamation was posted the President's address to the people. He proposed the election of a president for ten years. He referred the army to the neglect which it had received at the hands of former governments, and promised that the soldiery of France should rewin its ancient renown.

As soon as those members of the Assembly who had not been arrested could realize the thing which was done, they ran together and attempted to stay the tide of revolution by passing a vote deposing the President from office. But the effort was futile. A republican insurrection, under the leadership of Victor Hugo and a few other distinguished Liberals, broke out in the city. But there was in the nature of the case no concert of action, no resources behind the insurrection, and no military leadership. General Canrobert, Commandant of the Guards, soon put down the revolt in blood. Order was speedily restored throughout Paris, and the victory of the President was complete. It only remained to submit his usurpation to the judgment of the people, and the decision in that case could, under existing conditions, hardly be a matter of doubt.

In accordance with the President's proclamation, a popular election was held throughout France, on the twentieth and twenty-first of December, at which the Coup d'Etat was signally vindicated. Louis Napoleon was triumphantly elected President, for a period of ten years. Out of eight millions of votes, fewer than one million were cast against him. He immediately entered upon office, backed by this tremendous majority, and became Dictator of France. In January of 1852, sharp on the heels of the revolution which he had effected, he promulgated a new constitution. The instrument was based upon that of 1789, and possessed but few clauses to which any right-minded lover of free institutions could object. On the twenty-eighth of March, Napoleon resigned the dictatorship, which he had held since the Coup d'Etat, and resumed the office of President of the Republic.

It was not long, however, until the *After That* began to appear. Already in the summer and autumn of 1852 it became evident that the *Empire* was to be re-established. In the season of the vintage the President made a tour of the country, and was received with cries of *Vive L'Empereur*! In his addresses, particularly in that which he delivered at Bordeaux, the sentiment of Empire was cautiously offered to the people. The consummation was soon reached. On the seventh of November, 1852, a vote was passed by the French Senate for the re-establishment of the imperial order, and for the submission of the proposed measure to a popular vote.

The event showed conclusively that the French nation, as then constituted, was Bonapartist to the core. Louis Napoleon was almost unanimously elected to the imperial dignity. Of the eight millions of suffrages of France, only a few scattering thousands were recorded in the negative. Thus, in a blaze of glory that might well have satisfied the ambition of the First Bonaparte, did he, who, only twelve years before at Boulogne, had tried most ridiculously to excite a paltry rebellion by the display of a pet-eagle to his followers, mount the Imperial throne of France with the title of Napoleon III.

# THE CHARTIST AGITATION IN ENGLAND

One of the most important political movements of the present century was the Chartist agitation in Great Britain. This agitation began in 1838. It was an effort of the under man in England to gain his rights. In the retrospect, it seems to us astonishing that such rights as those that were then claimed by the common people of England should ever have been denied to the citizens of any free country. The period covered by the excitement was about ten years in duration, and during that period great and salutary reforms were effected, but they were not thorough, and to this day the under man in Great Britain is mocked with the *semblance* of political liberty, the *substance* of which he does not enjoy; the same is true in America.

The name *Chartist* arose from an article called the "People's Charter," which was prepared by the famous Daniel O'Connell. The document contained six propositions, follows:

(1) We demand Universal Suffrage—by which was meant rather Manhood Suffrage than what is now known as universal suffrage, meaning the ballot in the hands of both sexes. This the Chartists did not demand.

(2) We demand an Annual Parliament—by which was meant the election of a new House of Commons each year by the people.

(3) We demand the right to Vote by Ballot—by which was meant the right of the people to employ a *secret* ballot at the elections instead of the method *viva voce.*

(4) We demand the abolition of the Property Qualification now requisite as a condition of eligibility to Membership in the House of Commons.

(5) We demand that the Members of Parliament shall be paid a salary for their services.

(6) We demand the Division of the Country into Equal Electoral Districts—by which was meant an equality of *population*, as against mere territorial extent.

To the reader of to-day it must appear a matter of astonishment that the representatives of the working classes of Great Britain should have been called upon, at a time within the memory of men still living, to advance and advocate political principles so self-evident and common-sense as those declared in the Charter, and his wonder must be raised to amazement when he is told that the whole governing power of Great Britain, the King, the

Ministry, the House of Lords, the House of Commons, the Tories as a party, the Whigs as a party, and—all party divisions aside—the great Middle Class of Englishmen set themselves in horrified antagonism to the Charter and its advocates, as though the former were the most incendiary document in the world and the latter a rabble of radicals gathered from the purlieus of the French Revolution.

The reason for the outbreak of the Chartist reform was the fact that the Reform Bill of 1832 had proved a signal failure. For six years the English Middle Classes had sought by the agency of that act to gain their rights, but they had sought in vain. The people now began to follow popular leaders, who always arise under such conditions. One of these, by the name of Thorn, a bankrupt brewer and half madman, who called himself Sir William Courtenay, appeared in Canterbury. He said that he was a Knight of Malta and King of Jerusalem—this when he was only a knight of malt and a king of shreds and patches. Delusion broke out on every hand. One great leader was Feargus O'Connor. Another was Thomas Cooper, a poet, and a third was the orator Henry Vincent, afterward well known in America.

The agitation for reform spread far and wide. The people seemed to be about to rise *en masse*. The powers of British society were shaken and alarmed. The authorities put out their hands and the Chartist meetings in many places were broken up. The leading spirits were seized and thrown into prison for nothing. Three of the agitators were sent to the penal colonies, for no other offence than the delivery of democratic speeches. For several years the movement was in abeyance, but in 1848, in the month of April, the agitation broke out afresh and rose to a formidable climax. A great meeting was appointed for the Kensington common, and there, on the tenth of the month just named, a monster demonstration was held. A petition had meanwhile been drawn up, praying for reform, and was *signed by nearly two million Englishmen*!

After this the Chartist agitation ebbed away. The movement was said to be a failure; but it failed, not because of the political principles on which it was founded, but because those principles had in the meantime been acknowledged and applied. At least three of the six articles of the Chartist charter were soon adopted by Parliament. The principle of Manhood Suffrage is virtually a part of the English Constitution. The right of voting by Secret Ballot, deposited in a ballot-box, has also been acknowledged as a part of the *modus operandi* of all British elections. In like manner the Property Qualification formerly imposed on candidates for Parliament, against which the Chartists so vehemently and justly declaimed, has long since been abolished.

# THE ABOLITION OF HUMAN BONDAGE

Certainly no greater deed of philanthropy has been accomplished by mankind than the extinction of human servitude. True, that horrible relic of antiquity has not yet been wholly obliterated from the world, but the nineteenth century has dealt upon it such staggering and fatal blows as have driven it from all the high places of civilization and made it crouch in obscure corners and unenlightened regions on the outskirts of paganism. Slavery has not indeed been extinguished; but it is scotched, and must expire. According to the tendency of things, the sun in his course at the middle of the twentieth century will hardly light the hovel of a single slave!

The opening of the modern era found slavery universally distributed. There was perhaps at the middle of the eighteenth century not a single non-slave-holding race or nation on the globe! All were alike brutalized by the influences and traditions of the ancient system. All were familiar with it—aye, they were nursed by it; for it has been one of the strange aspects of human life that the children of the free have been nursed by the mothers of the enslaved. All races, we repeat, were alike poisoned with the venom of the serpent. Thus poisoned were France and Germany. Thus poisoned was England; and thus also our colonies. Time was, even down to the dawn of the Revolution, when every American colony was slave-holding. Time was when the system was taught in the schools and preached in the pulpits of all the civilized world.

It was about the Revolutionary epoch, that is, the last quarter of the eighteenth century, when the conscience of men began to be active on the subject of human bondage. We think that the disposition to recognize the wickedness and impolity of slavery was a part of the general movement which came on in civilization, tending to revolutionize not only the political but the social and ethical condition of mankind. We know well that in our own country, when our political institutions were in process of formation slavery was courageously challenged. It was not challenged more audaciously in the Northern than in the Southern colonies. Some of the latter, as, for example, Georgia, had at the first excluded slavery as a thing intolerable to freedom and righteousness. The leading men of the old Southern States at the close of the last century nearly all repudiated slavery in principle. They admitted it only in practice and because it was a part of their inheritance. The patriots, both North and South, were averse not only to the extension of the area of bondage, but to the existence of it as a fact.

Washington was at heart an anti-slavery man. He wished in his heavy but wholly patriotic way as heartily as Lincoln wished that all men might enjoy the blessings of freedom. Jefferson was almost radical on the question. Though he did not heartily believe in an overruling Providence, he felt the need of one when he considered the afflictive system of slavery with which his State and country were encumbered. He said that considering it he trembled when he remembered that God is just.

Meanwhile the unprofitableness of slavery in the Northern colonies had co-operated with the conscience of Puritanism to engender a sentiment against slavery in that part of the Union. So, although the institution was tolerated in the Constitution and even had guarantees thrown around it, it was, nevertheless, disfavored in our fundamental law. One may readily see how the patriots labored with this portentous question. Already in Great Britain an anti-slavery sentiment had appeared. There were anti-slavery leaders, statesmen, philosophers and philanthropists. By the terms of the Constitution the slave *trade* should cease in the year 1808. Sad to reflect that the inventive genius of man and the prodigality of nature in her gifts of cotton, sugar and rice to the old South should have produced a reaction in favor of slavery so great as to fasten it more strongly than ever upon our country.

The fact is, that to all human seeming at the middle of our century American slavery seemed to be more firmly established than ever before. Neither the outcry of the Northern abolitionists nor the appeals of Southern patriots such as Henry Clay, availed to check the pro-slavery disposition in fully one-half the Union, or to abate the covert favor with which the institution was regarded in nearly all the other half.

Meanwhile, however, slavery was suffering and expiring in nearly all parts of Europe. England began her battle against it even before the beginning of the century. The work of the philanthropists, begun as far back as 1786-87, when the Quakers, under the leadership of Clarkson and Sharpe, began to cry out against the atrocity of human bondage, now reached the public authorities, and ministers found it necessary to take heed of what the people were saying and doing. Both Pitt and Fox became abolitionists before the close of the eighteenth century. The first attack was against the slave *trade*. Bills for the abolition of this trade were passed in 1793-94 by the House of Commons, but were rejected by the Peers. In 1804 another act was passed; but this also was rejected by the Lords. So too, the bill of 1805! The agitation continued during 1806; and in 1807, just after the death of Fox, the slave trade *was* abolished in Great Britain.

The abolitionists went straight ahead, however, to attack slavery itself. The Anti-slavery Society was founded. Clarkson and Wilberforce and

Buxton became the evangels of a new order that was seen far off. It was not, however, until the great reform agitation of 1832 that the government really took up the question of the abolition of slavery. The bill for this purpose was introduced in the House of Commons on the twenty-third of April, 1833. The process of abolition was to be *gradual.* The masters were to be *compensated.* There were to be periods of apprenticeship, after which freedom should supervene. Twenty million pounds were to be appropriated from the national treasury to pay the expenses of the abolition process.

It was on the seventh of August, 1833, that this bill was adopted by the House of Commons. Two weeks afterward the House of Lords assented, and on the twenty-eighth of August the royal assent was given. The emancipation, however, was set for the first of August, 1834; and this is the date from which the abolition of slavery in Great Britain and her dependencies may be said to have occurred. In some parts, however, the actual process of extinguishing slavery lagged. It was not until 1843 that the 12,000,000 of slaves under British control in the empire were emancipated.

The virtual extinction of human slavery in the present century, presents a peculiar ethnical study. Among the Latin races, the French were the first to move for emancipation. It appears that the infusion of Gallic blood, as well as the large influence of the Frankish nations in the production of the modern French, has given to that people a bias in favor of liberty. All the other Latin races have lagged behind; but, France foreran even Great Britain in the work of abolition. Scarcely had the great Revolution of 1789 got under way, until an act of abolition conceding freedom to all men without regard to race or color was adopted by the National Assembly.

It was on the fifteenth of May, 1791, that this great act was passed. One of the darkest aspects of the character of Napoleon I. was the favor which he showed to the project of restoring slavery in the French colonies. But that project was in vain. The blow of freedom once struck produced its everlasting results. Though slavery lingered for nearly a half century in some of the French colonies, it survived there only because of the revolutions in the home government which prevented its final extinction. Acts were passed for the utter extirpation of the system during the reign of Louis Philippe, and again in the time of the Second Republic.

Meanwhile, the northern nations proceeded with the work of abolition. In Sweden slavery ceased in 1847. In the following year Denmark passed an Act of Emancipation. But the Netherlands did not follow in the good work until the year 1860. The Spaniards and Portuguese have been among the last to cling to the system of human servitude. In the outlying possessions of Spain, in Spanish America and elsewhere, the institution still maintains a precarious existence. In Brazil it was not abolished until 1871. In the Mohammedan countries it still exists, and may even be said to flourish. In Russia serfdom was abolished in 1863. He who at that date looked abroad over the world, might see the pillars of human bondage shaken, and falling in every part of the habitable globe which had been reclaimed by civilization.

In the meantime, Great Britain, in her usual aggressive way, had established an anti-slavery propaganda, from which strong influences extended in every direction. Her Anti-slavery Society re-established itself in the United States. Abolition candidates for the presidency began to be heard of and to be voted for at every quadrennial election. Such was Birney in 1844. Such (strange to say) was Martin Van Buren in 1848. Such four years afterward was John P. Hale, of New Hampshire, and such in 1856, as the storm came on, was John C. Fremont.

The political history of the United States shows at this epoch an astounding growth of anti-slavery sentiment; and this expanding force culminated in the election of Lincoln. Great, indeed, was the change which had already swept over the landscape of American thought and purpose since the despised Birney, in 1844, received only a few thousand votes in the whole United States. Now the Rail-splitter had come! The tocsin of war sounded. The Union was rent. War with its flames of fire and streams of blood devastated the Republic. But the bow of promise was set on the dark background of the receding storm. American slavery was swept into oblivion, and the end of the third quarter of the century saw such a condition established in both the New World and the Old, as made the restoration of human bondage forever impossible.

Not until the present order of civilization shall be destroyed will man be permitted again to hold his fellow-man in servitude. The chain that was said "to follow the mother," making all her offspring to be slaves; the manacles and fetters with which the weak were bound and committed to the mercies of heartless traders; all of the insignia and apparatus of the old atrocious system of bondage, have been heaped together and cast out with the rubbish and offal of the civilized life into the valley of Gehenna. There the whole shall be burned with unquenchable fire! Then the smoke, arising for a season, shall be swept away, and nothing but a green earth and a blue sky shall remain for the emancipated race of man.

# THE PERIL OF OUR CENTENNIAL YEAR

Americans are likely to dwell for a long time upon the glories of our Centennial of Independence. The year 1876 came and went, and left its impress on the world. Our great Exposition at Philadelphia was happily devised. We celebrated the one-hundredth anniversary of our independence, and invited all nations, *including Great Britain*, to join us in the festival. The Exposition was successful in a high degree. The nation was at its best. The warrior President who had led her armies to victory announced the opening and the close. Great things were seen. One or two great orations were pronounced, and in particular a great Centennial poem was contributed by that gifted son of genius, Sidney Lanier, of Georgia. Nor do we refrain from repeating, after twenty years, one of his poetic passages:

"Long as thine Art shall love true love;Long as thy Science truth shall know;Long as thine Eagle harms no Dove;Long as thy Law by law shall grow;Long as thy God is God above,Thy brother every man below,So long, dear Land of all my love,Thy name shall shine, thy fame shall glow!"

With the autumnal frost the great Exposition was concluded; and with that autumnal frost came a peril the like of which our nation had not hitherto encountered. The presidential election was held, and ended in a disputed presidency. We had agreed since the beginning of the century that ours should be a government by party. Against this policy Washington had contended stoutly; but after the death of the Father of his Country, the policy prevailed—as it has continued to prevail more and more to the present day.

In 1876 a Democratic reaction came on against the long-dominant Republican party, and Samuel J. Tilden, candidate of the Democracy, secured a *popular* majority. The *electoral* majority remained in dispute. Both parties claimed the victory. The election was so evenly balanced in its results—there had been so much irregularity in the voting and subsequent electoral proceedings in the States of Florida, Louisiana, South Carolina and Oregon, and the powers of Congress over the votes of such States were so vaguely defined under existing legislation—that no certain declaration of the result could be made. The public mind was confounded with perplexity and excitement, and there began to be heard the threatenings of civil war.

Perhaps the nation did not realize the danger; but the danger was present, and threatened to be overwhelming. The Republican party in possession of the Government was not willing to lose its advantage, and the Democratic party, declaring its majority to be rightful, was ready to rise in insurrection. As to the facts in the case, neither Samuel J. Tilden nor General R.B. Hayes was clearly elected to the presidency. The Democrats had carried two or three States by the persuasion of shotguns, and the Republicans with the aid of electoral commissions had counted in the electoral votes of a State or two which they did not carry at all. The excitement increased with the approach of winter, and it was proposed in a leading Democratic journal of the West that a hundred thousand Democrats should rise and march unarmed on Washington City, there to influence the decision of the disputed question.

When Congress convened in December, the whole question of the disputed presidency came at once before that body for settlement. The situation was seriously complicated by the political complexion of the Senate and the House of Representatives. In the former body the Republicans had a majority sufficient to control its action, while in the House the Democratic majority was still more decisive and equally willful.

At length the necessity of doing *something* became imperative. The great merchants and manufacturers of the country and the boards of trade in the principal cities grew clamorous for a peaceable adjustment of the difficulty. The spirit of compromise gained ground, and it was agreed to refer the disputed election returns to a joint high commission, to consist of five members chosen from the United States Senate, five from the House of Representatives, and five from the Supreme Court.

The judgment of this tribunal was to be final. The commission was accordingly constituted. The disputed returns were sent, State by State, to the High Court for decision. That body was itself divided politically, and *every member decided each question according to his politics.* The Republicans had seven votes in the court, the Democrats seven votes, and one vote, that of Judge Joseph P. Bradley, was said to be independent. But Judge Bradley was a Republican in his political antecedents, and whenever a question came to a close issue, he decided with his party.

On the second of March, only three days before the time for the inauguration, a final decision was reached. The Republican candidates were declared elected *by one electoral vote* over Tilden and Hendricks. Mr. Tilden had himself counseled peace and acquiescence. The decision was sullenly accepted by the Democrats, and the most dangerous political crisis in American history passed harmlessly by without violence or bloodshed. No patriot will care to see such a crisis come again.

# THE DOUBLE FETE IN FRANCE AND GERMANY

The Third Republic of France has passed its twenty-fifth anniversary, and the German Empire has just celebrated its semi-jubilee. The French held their fête in September of 1895, and on the eighteenth of the following January all the Fatherland shouted greetings to the grandson of old Wilhelm the Kaiser. The Gaul and the Teuton have thus agreed to be happy coincidently; but for very different reasons! The Gaul has his Republic and the Teuton his Empire. Side by side on the map lie the two great powers, representing in their history and present aspect one of the strongest contrasts to be found in human annals.

What the German Empire is we may permit the Emperor himself, in his recent anniversary address, to explain. His speech shows that Germany, of all civilized nations, has gone furthest in the direction of unqualified imperialism. The utterances of Emperor William surpass the speeches of the Czar himself, in avowing all the pretensions and fictions of monarchy in the Middle Ages. The Hohenzollern potentate openly makes the pretence of governing his subjects by rights and prerogatives in nowise derived from the people, but wholly derived from himself and his grandfather. Why should Germany be an Empire and France a Republic? How could such an amazing historical result come into the world? The French Republic and the new Empire of Germany were not made by generals and kings and politicians in 1870-71. Indeed, nothing is made by the strutters who are designated with such titles. The two great powers having their centres at Berlin and Paris have their roots as deep down as the subsoil of the ages. They grew out of antecedents older than the Crusades, older than Charlemagne, older than Augustus and the Christ. They came by law—even if the result *has* surprised the expectation of mankind.

When Cæsar made his conquest of Europe, he found the country north of the Alps in the possession of two races—both Aryan. These two races were as unlike then as they are now. The Gauls west of the Rhine were proper material for the reception of Roman rule; but the Germans beyond the Rhine were not receptive of any rule but their own. The Gallic races became Romanized. Gaul was a part of the Roman Empire and reasoning from the facts, we should have expected the Gaulish nations to develop into the imperial form.

For like reason we should expect the Teutonic races to develop into the greatest democracy of the modern world. Contrary to this double expectation, we have a French Republic and a German Empire. In 1870 the Gallic race became suddenly democratic, and at the same time the Germans became the greatest imperialists among civilized mankind! The German Empire has arisen where we should have expected a democracy; and the French Republic has arisen where we should have expected an Empire.

The illogical Empire lies alongside of the illogical Republic. They have a line of demarkation which, though drawn on the map, is not drawn on the ground. The great antagonistic facts touch each other through a long line of territorial extent, but the ethnic diversity does not permit political union. The Teuton and the Gaul continue to touch, but they are not one, and cannot be. Two neighbors living between Verdun and Metz are only a quarter of a mile apart. They cultivate their grounds in the same manner, raise the same fruits, have vines growing on the two sides of the same trellis. They speak the same language, exchange gossip and poultry; but their children do not go to the same school! One of them is a French democrat; the other, a German imperialist!

The reason for this reversal of expectation, by which the anticipated institutions of France are found in Germany and those of Germany in France, is this: It seems to be a law of human progress that mankind moves forward by reactions against its own preceding conditions; that is, Progress disappoints History *by doing the other thing*! The French race has done the other thing; and so has the German race! They who should have been logically the imperialists of Western Europe are the republicans and democrats. They who should have been logically the democrats and republicans of Europe—who should have converted Germania into the greatest democracy of the world—have accepted instead the most absolute empire. The phrase "German *Empire*" is, we think, the greatest paradox of modern history; and the phrase "French *Republic*" is another like it. But history has decreed it so; and the reason is that human progress works out its highest results by doing the other thing!

But this philosophical speculation or interpretation does not trouble either the French or the Germans. They both seem to rejoice at what has come to pass, and do not trouble themselves about the logistics of history. They celebrate their quarter centennials, the one for the Republic, and the other for the Empire, with profound enthusiasm, shouting, *Vive* for the one and *Hoch* for the other with an impulsive patriotism that has come down to them with the blood of their respective races from before the Christian era!

# Great Battles

# TRAFALGAR

Lord Byron in his celebrated apostrophe to the ocean could hardly omit a reference to the most destructive conflict of naval warfare within the present century. In one of his supreme stanzas he reserves Trafalgar for the climax:

"The armaments which thunderstrike the wallsOf rock-built cities, bidding nations quakeAnd monarchs tremble in their capitals,The oak leviathans, whose huge ribs makeTheir clay creator the vain title takeOf lord of thee and arbiter of war,—These are thy toys, and, as the snowy flake,They melt into thy yeast of waves, which marAlike the Armada's pride or spoils of Trafalgar."

The battle of Trafalgar, preceding by forty-two days the battle of Austerlitz, holds the same relation to British ascendancy on the ocean that Napoleon's victory over the Emperors Alexander and Francis held to the French ascendancy on Continental Europe. Henceforth Great Britain, according to her national hymn, "ruled the wave;" henceforth, until after Waterloo, France ruled the land. Up to this date, namely, 1805, French ambition had reached as far as the dominion of the sea. It appears that Napoleon himself had no genius for naval warfare, but his ambition included the ocean; coincidently with his accession to the Imperial throne a great fleet was prepared and placed under command of Admiral Villeneuve for the recovery of the Mediterranean.

This fleet was destined in the first place for a possible invasion of England, but fate and Providence had reserved for the armament another service. At the same time the British fleet, to the number of twenty-seven ships of the line and four frigates, was brought to a high stage of proficiency and discipline, and placed under command of Lord Horatio Nelson. His second in command was Admiral Collingwood, who succeeded him after his death. The French fleet was increased to thirty-three ships of the line and five frigates, the addition being the Spanish contingent under Admirals Gravina and Alava. The Spanish vessels joined Villeneuve from Cadiz about the middle of May. The plan of the French commander was to rally a great squadron, cross the Atlantic to the West Indies, return as if bearing down on Europe, and raise the blockades at Ferrol, Rochefort and Brest.

As soon as it was known, however, that Nelson was abroad, his antagonist became wary and all of his movements were marked with caution. Meanwhile Lord Nelson sought for the allied-fleet on the Mediterranean, but found it not. He then passed through the Straits of Gibraltar and sailed for the coast of South America; but before reaching his destination he learned that the Spanish fleet had sailed for Europe again. Nelson followed, but did not fall in with the enemy. Villeneuve, gaining knowledge of the movements of the English admiral, and disregarding the instructions of Napoleon, withdrew from Ferrol to the south and put in at Cadiz. It was here that Nelson, so to speak, brought the allied fleet to bay.

On the southern coast of Spain, between Cadiz and Gibraltar, the Cape of Trafalgar projects into the Atlantic. In the autumn Nelson's fleet beat southward into this part of the seas, and it was here that the battle was fought. The rival commanders were eager for a meeting, and each foresaw that the contest was likely to be decisive. Each admiral had behind him a long list of naval achievements, and each to his own nation was greatly endeared.

Nelson had, on the first of August, 1798, destroyed the French fleet in the bay of Aboukir. In 1800 he had been raised to the peerage. In 1801 he had bombarded Copenhagen; and for that doubtful achievement had been made a viscount. One of his arms was gone, and he was covered with the scars of battle. Villeneuve had also a well-earned reputation. Could he but add to his previous services the defeat of Nelson, his fame would be established for all time.

It was on the twenty-first of October, 1805, that the combined squadrons of France and Spain on the one side, and the fleet of Great Britain on the other, came face to face off the Cape of Trafalgar. The rocks of Gibraltar might be seen in the distance. The sea was calm and the sky clear. The combatants discerned in advance the greatness of the event that was at hand.

The conflict that ensued ranks among the great naval battles of the world. Lord Nelson, with all his heroism, was a vain man, capable of spectacular display. He clad himself in the insignia of the many orders to which he belonged, and might be conspicuously seen from the decks of the French ships. In fact, he seemed to court death almost as much as he strove for victory. In the beginning of the engagement he displayed from his pennon, where it might be read by the whole fleet, this signal: "England expects every man to do his duty."

On the display of this signal the British fleet rang with cheers. The shouting was heard as far as the opposing Armada. The tradition goes that Villeneuve said on hearing the shouts of the British marines: "The battle it lost already." The admirals of the allied fleet arranged their vessels in parallel lines, so that each ship of the rear line should break the space between two of the advanced line. This arrangement enabled all the ships to fire at once, and it was the purpose of Villeneuve to hold his vessels in this form so that the British squadron might gain no advantage from manoeuvring.

Nelson's arrangement, however, was quite different. His plan was to attack at two points and break through the Armada, throwing the ships into confusion right and left. This brought his own vessels into the arrangement of two harrows, each pointing the apex against the designated vessels of the opposing squadron. One of the harrows was to be led by Collingwood in his ship called the "Royal Sovereign." Nelson led his column in his flagship the "Victory." The preliminaries of the battle extended to noon, and then the British attack was begun by Collingwood, who bore down on the two opposing vessels, the "Santa Anna" and the "Fougeux." Nelson also sailed to the attack in the "Victory" and broke through the enemy's line between the "Redoubtable" and the "Santissima Trinidad." The "Victory" in passing poured terrible broad-sides into both vessels.

It seems that both the British admirals in going into battle outsailed somewhat their supporting ships; but these soon came into action and the battle line of the allied fleet was fatally broken at both points. All the vessels were soon engaged, and the rear line of Villeneuve gave way as well as the first. Nevertheless, the battle continued furiously for about two hours. The "Santissima Trinidad" was at that time the largest warship and the most formidable that had ever been built. The "Redoubtable" was only second in strength and equipment. Five or six others were men-of-war of the heaviest draught and metal. The French and Spanish soldiers fought bravely, going into the battle with flying streamers and answering shouts.

Nelson, utterly fearless, seems to have had a premonition of his fate. He had made a hasty codicil to his will, and entered the struggle to conquer or die. Both fates were reserved for him. From the beginning of the battle the French and Spanish ships suffered terribly from the British fire; but they also inflicted heavy losses on their assailants. Here and there a French vessel was shattered and fell out of the fight. Nelson was struck with a ball, but refused to go below. Again he was hit in the shoulder by a musketeer from the masts of the "Redoubtable" and fell to the deck. "They have done for me at last, Hardy," said he to Sir Thomas Hardy, captain of the ship. He was carried below by the officers, and as he lay bleeding the news was brought to him that already *fifteen* of the enemy's ships had surrendered. "That is well," said the dying hero; "but I had bargained for twenty." Then his thoughts turned to Lady Hamilton, to whom he was devoted. "Take care of Lady Hamilton, Hardy; take care of poor Lady Hamilton," said he, as the death dew dampened his brow. He then embraced the captain and expired.

The victory of the British fleet was complete. The allies lost nineteen ships. Admiral Gravina was killed, and Villeneuve was taken prisoner. He never reacted from the mortification of his defeat, but lingered until the following year, when he despaired of life and hope and committed suicide. Nelson, in the midst of a pageant hitherto unsurpassed, was buried in St. Paul's. The battle of Trafalgar passed into history as the first and greatest naval conflict of the century.

# CAMPAIGN OF AUSTERLITZ

The first four years of the present century were a lull before a tempest. These years covered on our side of the sea the administration of the elder Adams. In Europe they corresponded to the period of the transformation of the Consulate into the French Umpire. This change was rapidly and easily effected. The star of Napoleon emerged from the chaos and the cloud and rose rapidly to the zenith. But the mood of the age was war, war. Could Europe in these first years have foreseen the awful struggles that were just before, then Europe might well have shuddered.

Now it was that the ascendancy of the Corsican brought in a reign of violence and blood. Napoleon became the trampler of vineyards. His armies made Europe into mire. England—agreeing at Amiens not to fight—fought. Pitt, now in the last year of his life, used all of his resources to bring about a league against France. He persuaded Alexander of Russia, Francis of Austria, and Gustavus of Sweden—all easy dupes of a greater than themselves—to make a new coalition. He tried to induce Frederick William of Prussia to join his fortunes with the rest; but the last-named monarch was for the time restrained by the weakness of prudence. The agents of Napoleon held out to the king suggestions of the restoration of Hanover to Prussia. But Austria and Russia and Sweden pressed forward confidently to overthrow the new French Empire. That Empire, they said, should not see the end of the first year of its creation!

The Austrians were first in the field. The Russians, under Kutusoff, came on into Pomerania from the east. Out of Sweden, with a large army, came down Gustavus, the Don Quixote of the north, to crush Bernadotte, who held Hanover. Napoleon for his part sprang forth for the campaign of Austerlitz, perhaps the most brilliant military episode in the history of mankind. With incredible facility he threw forward to the Rhine an army of 180,000 men. His policy was—as always—to overcome the allies in detail.

On the twenty-fourth of September, the Emperor left Paris. The Empress and Talleyrand went with him as far as Strasburg. On the second of October, hostilities began at Guntzburg. Four days afterward the French army crossed the Danube. On the eighth of the month, Murat won the battle of Wertingen, capturing Count Auffenberg, with 2000 prisoners. On the tenth the French had Augsburg, and on the twelfth, Munich. On the fourteenth Soult triumphed at Memingen, capturing a corps of 6000 Austrians; and on the same day Ney literally overran the territory which was soon to become his Duchy of Elchingen. Napoleon out-generaled the main division of the enemy at Ulm. The Austrians, under General Mack, 33,000 strong, were cooped up in the town and, on the seventeenth of October, forced to capitulate. Eight field-marshals and generals, including the Prince Lichtenstein and Generals Klenau and Fresnel, were made prisoners. "Soldiers of the Grand Army," said Napoleon, "we have finished the campaign in a fortnight!"

On the day of the capitulation of Ulm, Massena in Italy drove back the army of the Archduke Charles. The Austrians to this date, in a period of twenty days, had lost by battle and capture fully fifty thousand men! On the twenty-seventh of October, the French army crossed the Inn. Saltzburg and Braunau were taken. In Italy, Massena, on the thirtieth, won the battle of Caldiero, and took 5000 prisoners. The French closed toward the Austrian capital. On the thirteenth of November, Napoleon, having obtained possession of the bridges of the Danube, entered Vienna. He established himself in the imperial palace of Schonbrunn. The Austrian Empire and the Holy Roman Empire—which was its shadowy penumbra—seemed to vanish like ghosts before him.

Out of Pomerania into Moravia, to the plain of Olmutz, the great Russian army under the Czar and Kutusoff, came roaring. There they were united with a heavy division of the Austrians, under the Emperor Francis. The latter had fled from his capital, and staked his last fortunes on a battle in the field. The allied army was 80,000 strong. Napoleon, with 60,000 men, commanded by Soult, Lannes, Murat and Bernadotte, advanced rapidly from the direction of Vienna, as far as Brunn, and there awaited the onset.

Just beyond this town, at Austerlitz, the French were arranged in a semicircle, with the convex front toward the allies, who occupied the outer arc on a range of heights. Such was the situation on the night of December 1, 1805. The morrow will be the first anniversary of our coronation in Notre Dame—a glorious day for battle!

With the morning of the second, Napoleon could scarcely restrain his ardor. The enthusiasm of the army knew no bounds. On the night before, the Emperor, in his gray coat, had gone the circle of the camps, and the soldiers, extemporizing straw torches to light the way, ran before him. Looking eagerly through the gray dawn, he saw the enemy badly arranged, or moving dangerously in broken masses under the cover of a Moravian fog. Presently the fog lifted, and the sun burst out in splendor. The onset of the French was irresistible. The allied centre was pierced. The Austrian and Russian emperors with their armies were sent flying in utter rout and panic from the field. Thirty thousand Russians and Austrians were killed, wounded and taken. Alexander barely escaped capture. Before sunset the Third Coalition was broken into fragments and blown away. At the conference between Napoleon and Francis, two days afterward, at the Mill of Sar-Uschitz, some of the French officers overheard the father of Maria Louisa lie to her future husband, thus: "I promise not to fight you any more."

# "FRIEDLAND—1807"

Whoever visits the Metropolitan Museum of Art in Central Park, New York, is likely to pause before a great historical painting by Jean Louis Ernest Meissonier. The picture is entitled "Friedland—1807." There goes a critical opinion that, though common fame would have Austerlitz to be the greatest battle of the Napoleonic wars, the palm ought really to be given to Friedland. At any rate, the martial splendor of that day has been caught by the vision and brush of Meissonier, and delivered, in what is probably the most splendid painting in America, to the immortality of art.

Let us note the great movements that preceded the climax of Friedland. In the summer of 1806, the historical conditions in Europe favored a general peace. Pitt was dead, and Fox agreed with Napoleon that a peace might now be secured by the restoration of Hanover to England. Suddenly, however, on the thirteenth of September, 1806, Fox died, and by the incoming of Lauderdale the whole complexion was changed. Toryism again ran rampant. The Anglo-Russo-Prussian intrigue was renewed, and the rash Frederick William sent a peremptory challenge to Napoleon to get himself out of Germany.

The Emperor had in truth agreed to withdraw his forces, but the Czar Alexander had also agreed to relinquish certain vantage grounds which he held—and had not done it. Therefore Napoleon's army corps would remain in Germany. Frederick William suddenly declared war, and in a month after the death of Fox, Napoleon concentrated in Saxe-Weimar an army of a hundred thousand men. Then, on the fourteenth of October, 1806, was fought the dreadful battle of Jena, in which the Prussians lost 12,000 in killed and wounded, and 15,000 prisoners. On the same day, Davout fell upon a division of 50,000 under the Duke of Brunswick and Frederick William in person, and won another signal victory which cost the Germans about ten thousand men.

Prussia was utterly overwhelmed by the disaster. Her fortresses were surrendered without resistance, and Napoleon, in less than a fortnight, occupied Berlin. On the twenty-first of November, he issued from that city his celebrated Berlin decree, declaring the British Islands in a state of blockade, and interdicting all correspondence and trade with England! The property of British subjects, under a wide schedule of liabilities, was declared contraband of war.

Meanwhile the aid promised to Prussia by the Czar had been too slow for the lightning that struck at Jena. The oncoming Russians reached the

Vistula, but were forced back by the victorious French, who took possession of Warsaw. There the Emperor established his winter quarters, and remained for nearly three months, engaged in the preparation of new plans of conquest and new schemes for the pacification of Europe.

After Jena, Prussia, though crushed, remained belligerent. Her shattered forces drew off to the borders, and were joined by the Russians in East Prussia. The campaign of 1807 opened here. On the eighth of February, the French army, about 70,000 strong, advanced against the allies, commanded by Benningsen and Lestocq. At the town of Eylau, about twenty miles from Königsberg, a great but indecisive battle was fought, in which each army suffered a loss of nearly eighteen thousand men. The Russians and Prussians fell back about four miles to Friedland, and both armies were reinforced, the French to about eighty thousand, and the allies to approximately the same number.

Here for a season the two great camps were pitched against each other. The shock of Eylau and the inclemency of the spring, no less than the political complications that thickened on every horizon, held back the military movements until the beginning of summer. But at length the crisis came. On the fourteenth of June was fought the great battle of Friedland and the allied army was virtually destroyed. The loss of the Russians and Prussians was more than twenty-five thousand men, while the French loss was not quite eight thousand. Napoleon commanded in person, and his triumph was prodigious.

Let not the visitor to the Metropolitan Museum fail to look long and attentively on the picture of the scene which represents the beginning of the battle on the side of the French. There on a slight elevation, in the wheatfield of June, sitting on his white horse, with his triangular hat lifted in silent salutation, surrounded by the princes and marshals of his Empire, sits the sardonic somnambulist, while before him on the left the Cuirassiers of the Guard, on their tremendous horses gathered out of Normandy, plunging at full gallop, bearing down through the broken wheat, with buglers in the van and sabers flashing high and bearded mouths wide open with yellings that resound through the world till now, charge wildly, irresistibly onward against the unseen enemy, reckless alike of life and death, but choosing rather death if only the marble face but smile!

# UNDER THE RUSSIAN SNOWS

The first empire of France was buried between the Niemen and Moscow. The funeral was attended by vultures and Cossacks.

It was on the twenty-fourth of June, 1812, that Napoleon began the invasion of Russia. The dividing line was the River Niemen. The inhabitants fell back before him. He had not advanced far when he encountered a new commander, with whom he was unfamiliar. It was Field-Marshal Nature. Marshal Nature had an army that the Old Guard had never confronted. His herald was Frost, and his aid-de-camp was Zero. One of his army corps was Snow. His bellowing artillery was charged with Lithuanian tempests. Hail was his grape and shrapnel. The Emperor of the French had never studied Marshal Nature's tactics—not even in the Alps.

The Russian summer was as midwinter to the soldiers of France and Spain and Italy. Some of the invading divisions could hardly advance at all. The howling storms made impassable the ungraded roads; the 1200 guns of the Grand Army sank into the mire. Horse-life and man-life fell and perished in the sleet of the mock-summer that raged along the watershed between the Dwina and the Dnieper.

The Russians under Kutusoff fell back to Smolensko. There on the sixteenth of August they fought and were defeated with a loss of nearly twelve thousand men. The way was thus opened as far as the Moskwa. At that place on the seventh of September Kutusoff a second time gave battle, at the village of Borodino. This was one of the most murderous conflicts of modern times. A thousand cannon vomited death all day. Under the smoke a quarter of a million of men struggled like tigers. At nightfall the French had the field. The defeated Russians hung sullenly around the arena where they had left more than 40,000 of their dead and wounded. The Frence losses were almost equally appalling. "Sire," said Marshal Ney, "we would better withdraw and reform." "*Thou* advise a retreat, Michel?" said the marble head, as it turned to the Bulldog of Battles.

Kutusoff abandoned Moscow. The inhabitants receded with him to the great plains eastward. On the fifteenth of September, Napoleon entered the ancient capital. The streets were as a necropolis. All was silence. The conqueror took up his residence in the old palace of the Czars. Here he would spend the winter in luxurious quarters. Here he would extemporize theatres, and here he would issue edicts as from Berlin and Milan. Lo, out of the Bazaar, near the Kremlin, bursts a volume of flame! The surrounding region is lighted with the glare. Moscow is on fire in a thousand places. The equinoctial gales fan the flame. For five days there is the roar of universal combustion. Then it subsides. But Moscow is a blackened ruin. Napoleon tries in vain to open negotiations with the Czar; but Alexander and Kutusoff will not hear. The French are left to enjoy the ashes of a burnt-up Russian city.

Already winter was at hand. The snow was falling. The soldier of fortune had at last found his destiny. On the nineteenth of October, he left Moscow, and the retreat of the Grand Army began toward the Niemen. Had the retreat been unimpeded, that army might have made its way back to France with comparatively trifling losses. Indeed the fame of having burnt the old capital of the Czars might have satisfied the conqueror with his expedition. But no sooner did he recede than the Cossacks arose on every hand, and assailed the fugitives. The soldiers of the West and South dropped and perished by thousands along the frozen roads. The ice-darts in their sides were sharper than Russian bayonets. A hundred and twenty thousand men rolled back horridly across the hostile world. The bridges of the Beresina break down under the retreating army, and in the following spring, when the ice-gorges go down the river, 12,000 dead Frenchmen shall be washed up from the floods!

There is constant battle on flank and rear. All stragglers perish. The army dwindles away. It is almost destroyed. Ney brings up the rear guard, wasted to a handful. At the passage of the Niemen, soiled with dirt, blackened with smoke, without insignia, with only drawn sword, and facing backward toward the hated region, the "Bravest of the Brave" crosses the bridge. He is the last man to save himself from the indescribable horrors of the Campaign of Russia.

The remnants of the Grand Army dragged themselves along until they found refuge in Königsberg. Napoleon had gone ahead toward France. After Moscow he took a sledge, and sped away across the snow-covered wastes of Poland, on his solitary journey to Paris. There is a painting of this scene by the Slavic artist Kowalski, which represents the three black horses abreast, galloping with all speed with the Emperor's sledge across the cheerless world which he traversed. He came to his own capital unannounced. None knew of his arrival until the next day. At four o'clock in the morning of that day, some one entered his office at the Tuileries, and found him with his war-map of Europe spread out on the floor before him. He was planning another campaign! In doing so, he could hardly forget that the Grand Army of his glory was under the Russian snows!

# WATERLOO

One battle in this century rises in fame above all other conflicts of the ages. It is Waterloo.

It was on the night of the seventeenth of June, 1815, that the British and French armies, drawing near each other on the borders of Belgium, encamped, the one near the little village of Waterloo and the other at La Belle Alliance. They were close together. A modern fieldpiece could easily throw a shell from Napoleon's headquarters over La Haie Sainte to Mont St. Jean, and far beyond into the forest. During the afternoon of the seventeenth, and the greater part of the night, there was a heavy fall of rain. On the following morning the ground was muddy. The Emperor, viewing the situation, was unwilling to precipitate the battle until his artillery might deploy over a dry field.

As to the temper of the Emperor, that was good. Hugo says of him: "From the morning his impenetrability had been smiling, and on June 18, 1815, this profound soul, coated with granite, was radiant. The man who had been sombre at Austerlitz was gay at Waterloo. The greatest predestined men offer these contradictions; for our joys are a shadow and the supreme smile belongs to God.

"'Cæsar laughs, Pompey will weep,' the legionaries of the Fulminatrix legion used to say. On this occasion Pompey was not destined to weep, but it is certain that Cæsar laughed.

"At one o'clock in the morning, amid the rain and storm, he had explored with Bertrand the hills near Rossomme, and was pleased to see the long lines of English fires illumining the horizon from Frischemont to Braine l'Alleud. It seemed to him as if destiny had made an appointment with him on a fixed day and was punctual. He stopped his horse and remained for some time motionless, looking at the lightning and listening to the thunder. The fatalist was heard to cast into the night the mysterious words, '*We are agreed.*' Napoleon was mistaken; they no longer agreed."

The arena of Waterloo is an undulating plain. Strategically it has the shape of an immense harrow. The clevis is on the height called Mont St. Jean, where Wellington was posted with the British army. Behind that is the village of Waterloo. The right leg of the harrow terminates at the hamlet of La Belle Alliance. The left leg is the road from Brussels to Nivelles. The cross-bar intersects the right leg at La Haie Sainte. The right leg is the highway from Brussels to Charleroi. The intersection of the bar with the left leg is near the old stone chateau of Hougomont. The battle was fought on the line of the cross-bar and in the triangle between it and the clevis.

The conflict began just before noon. The armies engaged were of equal strength, numbering about 80,000 men on each side. Napoleon was superior in artillery, but Wellington's soldiers had seen longer service in the field. They were his veterans from the Peninsular War, perhaps the stubbornest fighters in Europe. Napoleon's first plan was to double back the allied left on the centre. This involved the capture of La Haie Sainte, and, as a strategic corollary, the taking of Hougomont. The latter place was first attacked. The field and wood were carried, but the chateau was held in the midst of horrid carnage by the British.

Early in the afternoon a Prussian division under Billow, about 10,000 strong, came on the field, and Napoleon had to withdraw a division from his centre to repel the oncoming Germans. For two or three hours, in the area between La Haie Sainte and Hougomont, the battle raged, the lines swaying with uncertain fortune back and forth. La Haie Sainte was taken and held by Ney. On the whole, the British lines receded. Wellington's attempt to retake La Haie Sainte ended in a repulse. Ney, on the counter charge, called on Napoleon for reinforcements, and the latter at that moment, changing his plan of battle, determined to make the principal charge on the British centre, saying, however, "It is an hour too soon." The support which he sent to Ney was not as heavy as it should have been, but the Marshal concluded that the crisis was at hand, and Napoleon sought to support him with Milhaud's cuirassiers and a division of the Middle Guard. Under this counter charge the British lines reeled and staggered, but still clung desperately to their position. They gave a little, and then hung fast and could be moved no farther. In another part of the field Durutte carried the allied position of Papelotte, and Lobau routed Bülow from Planchenois. At half-past four everything seemed to portend disaster to the allies and victory to the French.

If the tragedy of Waterloo had been left at that hour to work out its own results as between France and England it would appear that the latter must have gone to the wall; but destiny had prepared another end for the conflict. Waterloo was a point of concentration. Several tides had set thither, and some of them had already arrived and broken on the rocks. Other tides were rolling in. The British wave had been first, and this had now been rolled back by the tide of France. A German wave was coming, however, and another French billow, either or both of which might break at any moment.

On the morning of June 18, at the little town of Wavre, fifteen miles southeast of Brussels and about eight or ten miles from Waterloo, a battle had been fought between the French contingent under Marshal Grouchy and the Prussian division under Thielmann, who commanded the left wing of Marshal Blücher's army. That commander had a force of fully forty thousand men under him, and was on his way to join his forces with those of Wellington on the plateau of Mont St. Jean. Grouchy had at this time between thirty and forty thousand men, and was under orders from Napoleon to keep in touch with his right wing, watching the Prussians and joining himself to the main army according to the emergency.

These two divisions—Blücher's and Grouchy's—were *sliding along* toward Waterloo, and on the afternoon of the eighteenth it became one of the great questions in the history of this century which would first arrive on the field. Napoleon believed that Grouchy was at hand. Wellington in his desperation breathed out the wish that either night or Blücher would come. The ambiguous result of the principal conflict made it more than ever desirable to both of the commanders to gain their reinforcements, each before the other. The event showed that the arrival of Bülow's contingent was really the signal for the oncoming of the whole Prussian army. The French Emperor, however, remained confident, and at half-after four he felt warranted in sending a preliminary despatch of victory to Paris.

Just at this juncture, however, an uproar was witnessed far to the right. The woods seemed to open, and the banners of Blücher shot up in the horizon. Grouchy was *not* on his rear or flank! Napoleon saw at a glance that it was then or never. His sun of Austerlitz hung low in the west. The British centre must be broken, or the empire which he had builded with his genius must pass away like a phantom. He called out four battalions of the Middle and six of the Old Guard. In the last fifteen years that Guard had been thrown a hundred times on the enemies of France, and never yet repulsed. It deemed itself invincible.

At seven o'clock, just as the June sun was sinking to the horizon, the bugles sounded and the finest body of horsemen in Europe started to its doom on the squares of Wellington. The grim horsemen rode to their fate like heroes. The charge rolled on like an avalanche. It plunged into the sunken road of O'Hain. It seemed to roll over. It rose from the low grounds and broke on the British squares. They reeled under the shock, then reformed and stood fast. Around and around those immovable lines the soldiers of the Empire beat and beat in vain. It was the war of races at its climax. It was the final death-grip of the Gaul and the Teuton. The Old Guard recoiled. The wild cry of "*La Garde recule*" was heard above the roar of battle. The crisis of the Modern Era broke in blood and smoke, and the past was suddenly victorious. The Guard was broken into flying squadrons. Ruin came with the counter charge of the British. Ney, glorious in his despair, sought to stay the tide. For an hour longer he was a spectacle to gods and men. Five horses had been killed under him. He was on foot. He was hatless. He clutched the hilt of a broken sword. He was covered with dust and blood. But his grim face was set against the victorious enemy in the hopeless and heroic struggle to rally his shattered columns.

Meanwhile the Prussians rushed in from the right. Wellington's Guards rose and charged. Havoc came down with the darkness. A single regiment of the Old Guard was formed by Napoleon into a last square around which to rally the fugitives. The Emperor stood in the midst and declared his purpose to die with them. Marshal Soult forced him out of the melee, and the famous square, commanded by Cambronne—flinging his profane objurgation into the teeth of the English—perished with the wild cry of "*Vive l'Empereur!*"

Hugo says that the panic of the French admits of an explanation; that the disappearance of the great man was necessary for the advent of a great age; that in the battle of Waterloo there was more than a storm, that is, the bursting of a meteor. "At nightfall," he continues, "Bernard and Bertrand seized by the skirt of his coat in a field near Genappe a haggard, thoughtful, gloomy man, who, carried so far by the current of the rout, had just dismounted, passed the bridle over his arm, and was now with wandering eye returning alone to Waterloo. It was Napoleon, the immense somnambulist of a shattered dream!"

On the spot where French patriotism afterward planted the bronze lion to commemorate forever the extinction of the Old Guard of the French Empire, and of Napoleon the Great, the traveler from strange lands pauses, at the distance of eighty years from the horrible cataclysm, and reflects with wonder how within the memory of living men human nature could have been raised by the passion of battle to such sublime heroism as that displayed in these wheatfields and orchards where the Old Guard of France sank into oblivion, but rose to immortal fame.

# SEBASTOPOL

In the fall of 1852 Louis Napoleon Bonaparte, Prince President of the French Republic, about to become the French Empire, was invited to a banquet by the Chamber of Commerce in Bordeaux. He was on his triumphal tour through the South of France. At the banquet he spoke, saying: "I accept with eagerness the opportunity afforded me by the Bordeaux Chamber of Commerce for thanking your great city for its cordial reception.... At present the nation surrounds me with its sympathies.... To promote the welfare of the country, it is not necessary to apply new systems, but the chief point above all is to produce confidence in the present and security for the future. For these reasons it seems France desires a return to the Empire. There is one objection to which I must reply. Certain minds seem to entertain a dread of war; certain persons say the Empire is only war. But I say *the Empire is peace.*"

The last four words of this extract became the motto of the Second Empire. Everywhere the Prince President's saying was blown to the world. "The Empire is peace" was published in the newspapers, echoed on the stage, and preached from the pulpits.

But the Empire was *not* peace. Just at this time Tennyson wrote his poem against France, as follows:

"There is a sound of thunder afar,Storm in the South that darkens the day—Storm of battle and thunder of war;Well if it do not roll our way!Form, form; riflemen, form!Ready, be ready to meet the storm!"

In less than a year the storm broke. It broke in Eastern Europe. Of the personal forces that brought the breaking, the two principal were the Czar Nicholas and the Emperor Louis Napoleon. In 1853 the Czar demanded of the Sultan certain guarantees of the rights of the Greek Christians in the Turkish provinces. This was refused, and the Crimean War broke out on the Danube. The first power in Western Europe to support the Sultan was France, while England and Sardinia came hard after. There was an alliance of England and France in support of the Turkish cause. In the bottom of the difficulty lay this question: Whether Russia might now move forward, gain control of the Black Sea, overawe the Porte, force her way through the Sea of Marmora into the Mediterranean, and thus rectify the mistake of Peter the Great in building his capital on the Gulf of Finland. All this and much more was called *The Eastern Question.*

The coast of the Black Sea became the seat of the war that ensued. The Russians posted themselves strongly in the Crimea. That peninsula was commanded by the famous fortress of Sebastopol, situated at the southwestern extremity. On the twenty-fifth of September, 1854, the heights of Balaklava, lying south of the fortress, were seized by a British division under command of Lord Raglan. In this way the Russians were besieged; for the allied fleets had made their way into the Black Sea, and the land side of Sebastopol was commanded by Balaklava.

The siege that ensued lasted for nearly eleven months, and was one of the most memorable of modern times. On two occasions the Russians sallied forth and gave battle. The first conflict of this kind was on the night of the twenty-fifth of October, 1854, at Balaklava. The Russian attack on the English and Turks was at first successful, and four redoubts were carried by the assailants. At the crisis of the battle, however, the British Highlanders came into action, and the Russians were repulsed. The latter did not attempt to renew the attack, but fell back into their intrenchments. It was at this juncture that the famous incident occurred of the Charge of the Light Brigade, which was immortalized by Tennyson in his poem.

A few days after the battle of Balaklava occurred another hard conflict at the village of Inkerman, at the head of the harbor of Sebastopol. On the fifth of November, 1854, a strong force of Russians descended from the heights, and were met by the allies on the slope opposite the ruins of an ancient town, which occupied the site in the times of Strabo. A severe battle ensued, in which the English and French were victorious. Many other sorties were made from the fortress, but were designed rather to delay the siege than with any serious hope of breaking the investment. Sometimes the conflicts, though desultory, were severe, taking the proportions of regular battles. But nothing decisive was effected, until winter closed on the scene, and brought upon both the besiegers and the besieged the greatest hardships.

The sufferings of the allies, so far away from the source of supplies, were at times beyond description. It is doubtful whether any other siege of modern times has entailed such cruel privations upon a civilized soldiery. At times the combined havoc of hunger, disease and cold was seen in its worst work in the allied camps. The genius of Elizabeth Butler has seized upon the morning "Roll Call," in the Crimean snows of 1855, as the subject of a great painting in which to depict the excess of human suffering and devotion—the acme of English heroism in a foreign land.

Meanwhile, the allied lines around Sebastopol were considerably contracted, and several serious assaults were made on the Russian works. On the twenty-third of February the French in front of the bastion, called the Malakhoff, assaulted that stronghold with great valor, but were unsuccessful. On the eighteenth of the following June an attempt was made to carry the Redan, a strong redoubt at the other extreme of the Russian defences, but the assailants were again repulsed. Then, on the sixteenth of August, followed the bloody battle of Tehernaya, in which the Russians made a final effort to raise the siege. With a force of 50,000 infantry and 6000 cavalry they threw themselves on the allied position, but were beaten back with great slaughter.

In the meantime, the trenches of the allies had been drawn so near the Russian works that there was a fair prospect of carrying the bastions by another assault. A terrible bombardment was begun on the fifth, and continued to the eighth of September, when both the Redan and the Malakhoff were taken by storm. But the struggle was desperate, and the losses on both sides immense. The Russians blew up their fortifications on the south side of the harbor, and retreated across the bay. Nor did they afterward make any serious attempt to regain the stronghold which the allies had wrested from them. The victors for their part proceeded to destroy the docks, arsenals and shipyards of Sebastopol, and, as far as possible, to prevent the future occupancy of the place by the Russians as a seat of commerce and war.

The siege and capture of Sebastopol virtually ended the contest, though the war lagged during the greater part of the ensuing year. On the second of March, 1855, the Czar Nicholas died, and Alexander II. came to the throne, predisposed to peace. It was not, however, until the thirtieth of March, 1856, that the Treaty of Paris was concluded, in which Russia was obliged to yield to the allied powers, among which France held the first place.

The story of the Crimean War, and of the siege of Sebastopol in particular, has passed into history as one of the great events, of the century. The struggles at Balaklava, on the river Alma, at Inkerman, and the storming of the Redan and the Malakhoff became the subjects of great historical paintings, of poems and of songs, the echoes of which are heard to the present day.

# SADOWA

From a military point of view, nothing in this century has been more brilliantly successful than the campaign of Prussia into Bohemia against the Austrians, culminating on the sixth of July, 1866, in the great conflict called the battle of Sadowa or Königgrätz—the one or the other from the two towns near which it was fought. The historical painter, Wilhelm Camphausen, of the School of Düsseldorf, has left among the art trophies of the world a painting of this battle which is as true to the field and the combatants as anything which we recall from the sublime leaves of historical art.

The scene represented is the triumphant conclusion of the battle. The field is wide and stormy. In the centre, riding at full gallop with his staff, is King William. Already he is receiving the cheers and salutations of victory. By his side are seen the stalwart figures of Bismarck, Von Roon, Von Moltke, the Crown Prince, Prince Frederick Charles, and many others destined in the ensuing ten years to rise to the heights of military fame. To the right of the group of commanders charges the column of the Uhlans. The Austrians before are broken, and falling into rout. Far to the left and in the distance may be seen the half-obscured wrecks of battle.

This conflict proved to be the Waterloo of Austria. It was the climax of the Seven Weeks' War. Already the Germans, under the leadership of Prussia, were making haste toward empire. The activity and energy displayed by the Prussian Government at this juncture were prodigious. It was like the days of Frederick the Great come again. The trouble with Austria had arisen about the claims of the Duke of Augustenburg to the government of Holstein. Bismarck desired that that duchy should be disposed of in one manner, while Austria was determined on another.

The German States were drawn into this controversy, and the support of Italy was sought by each of the contestants. Prussia held out to Italy the temptation of recovering Venice, as the reward of her entrance into a Prusso-Italian alliance. This bait was sufficient. The smaller German powers, with the exception of Oldenburg, Mecklenburg, the Saxon States, and three Free Cities, took their stand with Austria, and the German Diet approved of the Austrian demand. It looked for the time as though Prussia, with the exception of the aid of Italy, was to be left naked to all the winds of hostility. The event showed, however, that that great power was now in her element. She declared the action of the German Diet to be not only a menace, but an act of overt hostilities. This was followed by an immediate declaration of war against a foe that had nearly three times her numerical strength.

On the fifteenth of June, 1866, King William called upon Saxony, Hanover, Hesse-Cassel and Nassau to remain neutral in the impending conflict, and gave them *twelve hours* in which to decide! Receiving no answer, he ordered the Prussians out of Holstein to seize Hanover. This work was accomplished in two days. In another two days Hesse-Cassel was occupied by an army from the Rhine, while at the same time a third division of the Prussian forces was thrown into Dresden and Leipsic. On the twenty-seventh of the month, a battle was fought with the Hanoverians, in which the latter were at first successful, but were soon overpowered and compelled to surrender. George V., King of Hanover, fled for refuge to Vienna.

Within two weeks the field in the South was cleared, and the Prussian army was turned upon Austria. King William's forces numbered 260,000 men. They were commanded by the Crown Prince, Prince Frederick Charles, Von Moltke, Von Roon and General Bittenfeld. The King in person and Bismarck were present with the advance. The impact was more than Austria could stand. On the twenty-seventh and twenty-ninth of June, Frederick Charles defeated the Austrian advance in four indecisive engagements. Count Clam-Gallas, the Austrian general, was obliged to fall back on the main body for support.

In these same days the Crown Prince gained several preliminary successes over the principal Austrian army under Benedek. Then, on the river Bistritz, on the sixth of July, came the great battle of Sadowa. The opposing commanders in the beginning of the engagement were Frederick Charles and Benedek. The battle began at eight in the morning, and raged with the utmost fury until two in the afternoon. Thus far the Prussians had gained but little advantage; but at that hour the powerful division of the Crown Prince, which, like that of Blücher at Waterloo, had been delayed by recent rains, appeared on the Austrian right. The wing of Benedek's army was soon turned. Bittenfeld then broke the left, and under a general advance of the Prussian lines the Austrian centre gave way in confusion. The field was quickly swept. The overthrow of the Austrian army became a ruinous rout, and the out-flashing sun of evening looked upon a demoralized and flying host, scattering in all directions before the victorious charges of the Prussian cavalry.

The overwhelming victory of the Prussians was not without its rational causes. Indeed the antecedents of victory may always be found if all the facts of battle are known and analyzed. It remained for the battle of Sadowa to demonstrate practically the superiority of the needle-gun. This arm had been adopted by the Prussian government and was now for the first time on a great scale brought to the crucial test. Hitherto the old plan of muzzle-loading had been followed by all the nations of Europe and America. In our country the Civil War had come almost to its climax before breech-loading was generally introduced. Austria had continued to use the old muzzle-loading muskets. It seems surprising that nations, of whom intelligence and self-interest may well be predicated, should continue in such a matter as war to employ inefficient weaponry long after a superior arm has been invented.

If one might have looked into the gunshop of M. Pauli at Paris in the year 1814, he might have seen a gunsmith, twenty-seven years of age, plying his trade under the patronage of Napoleon the Great. That gunsmith was Johann Nicholas Von. Dreyse, of Sömmerda, who presently became an inventor as well as a smith, and in 1824, having returned to his own country, he took a patent for a new percussion method in musketry. Three years afterward he invented a needle-gun, retaining the muzzle-loading method. He continued his experimentation until 1836, when he made and patented the first breech-loading needle-gun complete. This was done under the patronage of the Prussian government. It was not until 1841, however, that this arm began to be supplied for Prussian troops, and it was twenty-five years after that date before the general adoption of this arm contributed to the rout of the Austrians at Sadowa.

The Prussians being armed with needle-guns, were enabled to get the double advantage of rapid firing by loading in a chamber at the breech of the piece, and the equally great advantage of a long range and most deadly missile; for in the cartridge of this gun the needle runs through the charge, firing it first at the front of the chamber, thus securing the whole force of the explosive, which burns backward in the enclosed space and expends itself entirely on the projectile. Those breech-loading pieces which fire the cartridge by percussion against its back end have the disadvantage of the charge burning forward, and thus wasting itself partly in the air after the bullet has left the muzzle. This difficulty, however, has been overcome in recent gunnery, and the needle-gun such as it was in the hands of King William's soldiers at Sadowa, must now be regarded as a clumsy and obsolete weapon.

The battle of Sadowa was to Francis Joseph the handwriting on the wall; but he made vain exertions to save his tottering fabric. Now it was that the shadow of a great hand was seen behind the conflict. It was the hand of Bismarck. His scheme was the unification of Germany. The NORTH GERMAN UNION was formed on the basis of Protestantism and the unity of the German race. Already the Empire might be seen in the distance.

# CAPTURE OF MEXICO

Whatever may be said of the justice of our war with Mexico, no criticism can be offered as to the brilliancy of the result. The campaign of General Scott against the ancient capital of the Aztecs, was almost spectacular; certainly it was heroic.

On the ninth of March, 1847, the General, then nearly sixty-one years of age, arrived at Vera Cruz, with an army of 12,000 men. That city was taken in about a week, and the way was opened from the coast to the capital. The advance began on the eighth of April, and ten days afterward the rocky pass of Cerro Gordo was carried by assault. Santa Anna barely escaped with his life, leaving behind 3000 prisoners, his chest of private papers, and his *wooden leg!*

On the twenty-second of the same month, the strong castle of Perote, crowning a peak of the Cordilleras, was taken without resistance. Then the sacred city of Puebla was captured. On the seventh of August, Scott, with his reduced forces, began his march over the crest of the mountains against the city of Mexico. The American army, sweeping over the heights, looked down on the valley. Never before had a soldiery in a foreign land beheld a grander scene Clear to the horizon stretched a living landscape of green fields, villages, and lakes—a picture too beautiful to be marred with the dreadful enginery of war.

The American army advanced by the way of Ayotla. The route was the great national road from Vera Cruz to Mexico. The last fifteen miles of the way was occupied with fortifications, both natural and artificial, and it seemed impossible to advance directly to the gates of the city. The army was accordingly brought around Lake Chalco, and thence westward to San Augustine. This place is ten miles from the capital. The approach now lay along causeways, across marshes and the beds of bygone lakes. At the further end of each causeway, the Mexicans had built massive gates. There were almost inaccessible positions at Contreras, San Antonio and Molino del Rey. Further on toward the city lay the powerful bulwarks of Churubusco and Chapultepec. The latter was of great strength, and seemed impregnable. These various outposts were held by Santa Anna with a force of fully thirty thousand Mexicans.

The first assaults of the Americans were made on the nineteenth of August, by Generals Pillow and Twiggs. The line of communications between Contreras and Santa Anna's army was cut, and in the darkness of the following night an assault was made by General Persifer F. Smith, who about sunrise carried the place and drove the garrison pell-mell. This was the *first* victory of the memorable twentieth of August.

A few hours later, General Worth compelled the evacuation of San Antonio. This was the *second* victory. About the same time, General Pillow advanced on Churubusco, and carried one of the heights. The position was taken by storm, and the enemy scattered like chaff. This was the *third* triumph. The division of General Twiggs added a *fourth* victory by storming and holding another height of Churubusco, while the *fifth* and last was achieved by General Shields and Pierce, who drove back an army of reinforcements under Santa Anna. The Mexicans were thus forced back into the fortifications of Chapultepec.

On the following morning, the alarm and treachery of the Mexican authorities were both strongly exhibited. A deputation came out to negotiate; but the intent was merely to gain time for strengthening the defences. The terms proposed by the Mexicans were preposterous when viewed in the light of the situation. General Scott, who did not consider his army vanquished, rejected the proposals with scorn. He, however, rested his men until the seventh of September before renewing hostilities. On the morning of the eighth, General Worth was thrown forward to take Molino del Rey and Casa de Mata, which were the western defences of Chapultepec. These places were defended by about fourteen thousand Mexicans; but the Americans, after losing a fourth of their number in the desperate onset, were again victorious. The batteries were now turned on Chapultepec itself, and on the thirteenth of September that frowning citadel was carried by storm. This exploit opened an avenue into the city. Through the San Cosine and Belen gates the conquering army swept resistlessly, and at nightfall the soldiers of the Union were in the suburbs of Mexico.

During the night, Santa Anna and the officers of the Government fled from the city, but not until they had turned loose from the prisons 2000 convicts, to fire upon the American army. On the following morning, before day-dawn, a deputation came forth from the city to beg for mercy. This time the messengers were in earnest; but General Scott, wearied with trifling, turned them away with disgust. "*Forward!*" was the order that rang along the American lines at sunrise. The war-worn regiments swept into the beautiful streets of the famous city, and at seven o'clock the flag of the United States floated over the halls of the Montezumas. It was the triumphant ending of one of the most brilliant and striking campaigns of modern history.

The American army, as compared with the hosts of Mexico, had been but a handful. The small force which had left Vera Cruz on the march to the capital had lost considerably by battle and disease. Many detachments had been posted *en route* to hold the line of communications, and for garrison duty in places taken from the enemy. The army had thus dwindled until, after the battles of Churubusco and Chapultepec, *fewer than six thousand men* were left to enter and hold the capital.

The invasion had been remarkable in all its particulars. The obstacles which had to be overcome seemed insurmountable. There were walled cities to be taken, fortified mountain passes to be carried by storm, and frowning castles with cannon on the battlements to be assaulted by regiments whose valor and impetuosity were their only protection and warrant of victory. Yet the campaign was never seriously impeded. No foot of ground once taken from the Mexicans was yielded by false tactics or lost by battle.

The army which accomplished this marvel, penetrating a far-distant and densely peopled country, held by a proud race, claiming to be the descendants of Cortes and the Spanish heroes of the sixteenth century, and denouncing at the outset the American soldiers as "barbarians of the North," was, in large part, an army of volunteers—a citizen soldiery—which had risen from the States of the Union and marched to the Mexican border under the Union flag.

# VICKSBURG

The story goes that on a certain occasion some friends of General Grant, anxious to make him talk about himself—something he would hardly ever do—said: "General, at what time in your military career did you perceive that you were the coming man—that you were to have the responsibility and fame of the command-in-chief and end the war?" For little while the General smoked on, and then said, "*After Vicksburg!*"

Certain it is that the star of Grant, long obscured and struggling through storm and darkness, never emerged into clear light, rising in the ascendant, until after the capture of the stronghold of the Confederates on the Mississippi. After that it rose, and rose to the zenith.

The position of Vicksburg is hard to understand. The river at this place makes a bend to the north and then turns south again, leaving a delta, or peninsula, on the Louisiana side. Vicksburg occupies a kind of shoulder on the Mississippi side. The site is commanding. The river flows by the bluffs, as if to acknowledge its subjection to them. From the beginning of the war the Confederate authorities recognized the vast importance of holding this key to the great inland artery, and the Federal Government saw the necessity of clutching it from the enemy.

The mouth of the Mississippi was soon regained by the Government, so that there was no serious obstruction as far north as where the northern border of Louisiana crosses the river. From the north the Federal fleets and land forces made their way along the Tennessee border, and then the Arkansas border; but in the middle, between the twenty-second and thirty-third parallels, the Confederates got a strong grip on the Father of Waters, and would not relinquish their hold. Jackson, the capital of the State, was in their power also, and from Jackson eastward the great thoroughfare extended into Alabama, and thence expanded in its connections into all the Confederacy. From Jackson to Vicksburg reached the same line of communications, so that here, at Vicksburg, the Confederate power, having its seat in Richmond and its energy in the field, reached directly to the Mississippi river, and laid upon that stream a band of iron which the Union must break in order to pass.

Such was the situation at the beginning of 1863. General Grant, who had been under a cloud since Shiloh, had gradually regained his command, and to him fell the task of breaking the Confederate hold on the great river. He has himself in his *Memoirs* told the story of the Vicksburg campaign. He managed, by herculean exertions, to get his forces below Vicksburg, and then began his campaign from Grand Gulf inland toward the line of communication between Jackson and Vicksburg. It was some time before the Confederates took the alarm. When they did become alarmed about Grant's movements, General J.E. Johnston, who commanded at Jackson, and General J.C. Pemberton, who was in command at Vicksburg; made the most unwearied efforts to keep open the line of communications upon which the safety of Jackson and the success of Pemberton depended.

But Grant pressed on in a northwesterly direction until he came upon Pemberton in a position which he had chosen at Champion's Hill. Here, without doubt, was fought one of the critical battles of the Union war. If General Pemberton had been successful, that success would seem to have portended the end of Grant's military career. But a different fate was reserved for the combatants. Grant's army was strong, and had become seasoned by hardship into the veteran condition. His under officers—Logan, McPherson, Hovey, McClernand and A.J. Smith—were in full spirit of battle. The engagement was severely contested. The Union army, actually engaged, numbered 15,000, and Pemberton's forces were about equal in number; but the latter were disastrously defeated. The losses were excessive in proportion to the numbers engaged.

The Confederates now fell back to Big Black river. Their line of communication with Jackson was cut. A second battle was fought at Big Black River, and then, on the eighteenth of May, the victorious Union army surrounded Vicksburg, and the siege was begun. The siege lasted forty-seven days, and was marked by heroic resistance on the one side and heroic pertinacity on the other, to the degree of making it one of the memorable events in the military annals of the world. Gradually the Union lines were narrowed around the doomed town. Ever nearer and nearer the lines of riflepits were drawn. Day by day the resources of the Confederates were reduced. But their defences were strong, and their courage for a long time unabated.

General Pemberton hoped and expected that an attack on Grant's rear would be made in such force as to loosen his grip, and to enable the besieged to rise against the besiegers and break through. The Confederates, however, had not sufficient forces for such an enterprise. General Lee, in the East, had now undertaken the campaign of Gettysburg, and the Confederacy was already strained in every nerve. General Grant had the way open for supplies and re-enforcements. The siege was pressed with the utmost vigor, and Pemberton was left to his fate.

Meanwhile, however, two unsuccessful assaults were made on the Confederate works. The first of these occurred on the day after the investment was completed. It was unsuccessful. The Union army was flung back from the impregnable defences in the rear of Vicksburg, and great losses were inflicted on them. Grant, however, was undismayed, and, still believing that the enemy's line might be broken by assault, renewed the attempt in a gallant attack on the twenty-second of May. A furious cannonade was kept up for several hours, and then the divisions of Sherman, McPherson and McClernand were thrown forward upon the earthworks of the enemy.

It was here that General McClernand reported to the commander that he had gained the Confederate intrenchments. General Grant says: "I occupied a position from which I thought I could see as well as he what took place in his front; and I did not see the success he reported. But his request for reinforcements being repeated, I could not ignore it, and sent him Quinby's division. Sherman and McPherson were both ordered to renew their assaults in favor of McClernand. This last attack only served to increase our casualties, without giving any benefit whatever." In these attacks large numbers of the Federal soldiers had got into the low ground intervening, under the enemy's fire, and had to remain in that position until darkness enabled them to retire. The Union losses were very heavy, and General Grant, years afterward, in composing his *Memoirs*, referred to this assault and to that at Cold Harbor as the two conspicuous mistakes of his military career.

Now it was that the regular siege of Vicksburg was undertaken. Toward the latter part of June, the Confederates, both soldiers and citizens, began to suffer. Houses became untenable. The people sought what refuge they might find. Some actually burrowed in the earth. The garrison was placed on short rations, and then a condition of starvation ensued. Pemberton held out with a resolution worthy of a better fate. But at length human endurance could go no further. On the fourth of July the white flag was hoisted from the Confederate works, announcing the end. Generals Grant and Pemberton, with three or four attendants each, met between the lines, and the terms of capitulation were quickly named and accepted. Vicksburg was surrendered. General Pemberton and all his forces, 30,000 strong, became prisoners of war.

This was the greatest force ever surrendered in America, though it was only about one-sixth of that of Marshal Bazaine and his army at Metz seven years afterward. Thousands of small arms, hundreds of cannon, and all the remaining ammunition and stores of the Confederates were the other fruits of this great Union victory, by which the prospect of ultimate success to the Confederacy was either destroyed or long postponed, and by which in particular the great central river of the United States was permitted once more to flow unvexed from the confluence of the Missouri to the Gulf.

# GETTYSBURG

The battle of Gettysburg is properly included among the great battles of the world. It was the greatest conflict that has thus far occurred in America. The losses relative to the numbers engaged were not as great as those at Antietam, Spottsylvania, and a few other bloody struggles of our war; but in the aggregate the losses were greatest. Gettysburg was in truth the high tide of the American Civil War. Never before and never afterward was there a crisis such as that which broke in the dreadful struggle for the mastery of Cemetery Ridge.

The invasion of the Northern States by General Lee had been undertaken at the close of the previous summer. That invasion had ended disastrously at the battle of Antietam. Once more the Confederate commander would make the trial. So well had he been able to beat back every invasion of Virginia by the Union forces that he now thought to end the war by turning its tide of devastation into Pennsylvania.

Doubtless Lee realized that he was placing everything upon the cast of a die. He undertook the campaign with a measure of confidence. He, almost as much as Grant, was a taciturn man, not much given to revelations of his purposes and hopes. No doubt he was somewhat surprised at the successful rising of the Union forces against him. Besides the Army of the Potomac, Pennsylvania seemed to rise for the emergency.

It has not generally been observed that before the great battle General Meade was in a position seriously to threaten the Confederate rear. Armies in the field rarely meet each other at the place and time expected. There is always something obscure and uncertain in the oncoming of the actual conflict. The fact is that General Lee was receding somewhat at the time of the crisis. Then it was that he determined to fight a great battle, and if successful then march on Washington. Should he not be successful, he would keep a way open by direct route for retreat into Virginia.

By the first of July, 1863, a situation had been prepared which signified a decisive battle with far-reaching consequences to the one side or the other, accordingly as victory should incline to this or to that. By this date General Reynolds, who commanded the advance line of the Union army, met the corresponding line of the Confederates at the village of Gettysburg, and the rest followed as if by logical necessity.

On July 1 and 2, the great body of the Union and Confederate armies came up to the position where battle had already begun between the advance divisions and the pressure of the one side upon the other became greater and greater with each hour. At the first the Confederate impact was strongest. General Reynolds was killed. Reinforcements were hurried up on both sides. General Howard, who succeeded Reynolds, selected Cemetery Hill, south of the town of Gettysburg, and there established the Union line.

General Meade arrived on the field on the afternoon of the first, and the two armies were thrown rapidly into position. That of the Federals extended in the form of a fishhook from Little Round Top by way of Round Top and along Cemetery Ridge through the cemetery itself, by the way of the gate, and then bending to the right, formed the bowl of the hook, which extended around as far as Culp's Hill and Wolf Creek. The ground was elevated and the convexity was toward the enemy.

By nightfall of the first, both armies were in state of readiness for the conflict. The Union army was on the defensive. It was sufficient that it should hold its ground and repel all assault. The Confederates must advance and carry the Federal position in order to succeed. How this should be done was not agreed on by the Confederate commanders. General Lee formed a plan of direct assault; but General Longstreet was of opinion that a movement of the army to the Union left flank would be preferable, and that by that method the flank might be turned and the position of Meade carried with less loss and much less hazard.

Longstreet, however, did not oppose the views of his commander to the extent of thwarting his purpose or weakening the plan adopted. On the second of July the battle began in earnest about noon. The Confederates advanced against the Union centre and left, and at a later hour a strenuous and partly successful attack was made on the Federal right. But complete success was not attained by Lee in any part of the field. About sundown the Confederates gained considerable advantage against Slocum, who held the line along Wolf Hill and Rock Creek; and on the Union left a terrible struggle occurred for the possession of Great and Little Round Top. In this part of the field the fighting continued until six o'clock in the evening; but the critical positions still remained in the hands of the Federals.

In the centre the contest was waged for the mastery of Cemetery Hill, which was the key to the Union position. Here were planted batteries with an aggregate of eighty guns, and here, though the assaults of the Confederates were desperate and long continued, the integrity of the Federal line was preserved till nightfall. The fighting along a front of nearly five miles in extent continued in a desultory manner until about ten o'clock on the July night, when the firing for the most part ceased, leaving the two armies in virtually the same position which they had occupied the day before.

This signified, however, that thus far the advantage was on the Union side; for on that side the battle was defensive. The Confederate army had come to a wall, and must break through or suffer defeat. The burden of attack rested on the Confederate side; but General Lee did not flinch from the necessity. In the darkness of night both he and the Union commanders made strenuous preparations for the renewal of the struggle on the morrow.

On the morning of the third both armies seemed loath to begin the conflict. This phenomenon is nearly always witnessed in the case of really critical battles. It was so at Waterloo, and so at Gettysburg. It seems that in such crises the commanders, well aware of what is to come, wait awhile, as though each would permit the other to strike first. As a matter of fact, the topmost crest of the Civil War had now been reached; and from this hour the one cause or the other must decline to the end.

The whole forenoon of the third of July was spent in preparations. There was but little fighting, and that little was desultory. At midday there seemed to be a lull along the whole line. Just afterward, however, General Lee opened from Seminary Ridge with about one hundred guns, directing his fire against the Union centre on Cemetery Hill. There the counter position was occupied by the American artillery of about equal strength, under command of General Hunt. The cannonade burst out at one o'clock with terrific roar. Nothing like it had ever before been seen or heard in the New World. Nothing like it, we believe, had ever up to that time been witnessed in Europe. Certainly there was no such cannonade at Waterloo. For about an hour and a half this tremendous vomit of shot and shell continued. It was the hope of General Lee to pound the Union batteries to pieces, and then, while horror and death were still supreme in the Union centre, to thrust forward an overwhelming mass of his best infantry into the gap, cut Meade's army in two, plant the Confederate banner on the crest of the Union battle line, and virtually then and there achieve the independence of the Confederate States.

It seems that an action of General Hunt, about half-past two, flattered Lee with the belief that he had succeeded. Hunt adopted the plan of drawing back his batteries over the crest of the hill, for the double purpose of cooling his guns that were becoming overheated and of saving his supply of ammunition, that was running low. The Union fire accordingly slackened and almost ceased for a while. Nor was Lee able to discover from his position but what his batteries under General Alexander had prevailed. It looked for the moment as though the battle were lost to Meade, and that victory was in the clutch of his antagonist.

Already a Confederate charge of infantry had been prepared. About 18,000 men, in three divisions, under Armistead, Garnett and Pettigrew, and led by General George E. Pickett, of Virginia, had been got into readiness for the crisis which had now arrived. Longstreet was the corps commander, and through him the order for the charge should be given. General Lee had himself made the order, but Longstreet seeing, as he believed the inevitable, hesitated and turned aside. It was not a refusal to send an army to destruction, but the natural hesitation of a really great commander to do what he believed was fatal to the Confederate cause. Pickett, however, gave his salutation to Longstreet, and presently said: "Sir, I am going to move forward!"

Then began the most memorable charge ever witnessed in America. The Confederate column was three-fourths of a mile in length. It was directed against the Union centre, where it was supposed the Confederate fire had done its work. What ensued was the finest military spectacle that had been seen in the world since the charge of the Old Guard at Waterloo; and the results were alike! The brave men who made the onset were mowed down as they crossed rapidly the intervening space. Hunt's batteries were quickly run back to their position, and began to discharge their deadly contents against the head of the oncoming column. That column veered somewhat to the right as it came. The line staggered, but pressed on. It came within the range of the Union musketry. Gaps opened here and there. Armistead, who led the advance, saw his forces sink to the earth; but he did not waver. Nearer and nearer the column came to the Union line. It *struck* the Union line. There was a momentary melee among the guns, and then all was over. Hancock's infantry rose with flash on flash from among the rocks by which they were partially protected. The Confederates were scattered in broken groups. Retreat was well-nigh impossible. The impact of the charge was utterly broken, and the Confederate line was blown into rout and ruin. Victory hovered over the National army. The Confederate forces staggered away under the blow of defeat. Night came down on a broken and virtually hopeless cause. The field was covered with the dead and dying. Two thousand eight hundred and thirty-four Union soldiers had been killed outright; 13,709 were wounded, and 6643 were missing, making a total of 23,186 men. The Confederate loss was never definitely ascertained, but was greatly in excess of that of the Federals. The best estimate has been fixed at 31,621. The grand total of losses in those fatal three days thus reached the enormous aggregate of 54,807!

# SPOTTSYLVANIA

A losing cause never showed a braver front than the Confederacy put on in the Wilderness. It was a front of iron. A man weaker than Grant would have quailed before it. It was virtually the same old rim of fire and death that had confronted McClellan, that had consumed Pope, that almost destroyed both Hooker and Burnside. Either the Union army must go through this barrier of flame and destruction and scatter it like brands of fire to right and left, or else the Union could never be rebuilded on the foundation of victory.

There was much discussion—and some doubt—in the spring of 1864 whether the Silent Man of Galena, now made Commander-in-chief of the Union armies, could pursue his military destiny to a great fame with Robert E. Lee for his antagonist. This talk was bruited abroad; Grant himself heard it, and had to consider what not a few people were saying, namely, that he had had before him in the West as leaders of the enemy only such men as Buckner and Beauregard and Pemberton; now he must stand up face to face with "Old Bobby Lee" and take the blows of the great Virginian against whom neither strategy nor force had hitherto prevailed.

The Man of Galena did not quail. Neither did he doubt. His pictures of this epoch show him with mouth more close shut than ever; but otherwise there was no sign. Lee for his part knew that another foeman was now come, and if we mistake not he divined that the end of the Confederacy, involving the end of his own military career, was not far ahead. It is to the credit of his genius that he did not weaken under such a situation and despair ere the ordeal came upon him; but on the contrary, he planted himself in the Wilderness and awaited the coming of the storm.

Let the world know that Grant in entering upon his great campaign, in the first days of May, 1864, had to do so against the greatest disadvantages. The country south of the Rappahannock was against him. The fact of Lee's acting ever on the defensive was against him. The woods and the rivers were against him. All Virginia, from the Rapidan to Richmond, was a rifle-pit and an earthwork. The Confederates knew every hill and ravine as though they were the orchard and the fishing creek of their own homes. The battlefield was theirs, to begin with; it must be taken from them or remain theirs forever. To take a battlefield of their own from Virginians has never been a pleasing task to those who did it—or more frequently tried to do it and did not!

It remained for Grant and his tremendous Union army to undertake this herculean task. He moved into the Wilderness and fought a two-days' battle of the greatest severity. The contest of the fifth and sixth of May were murderous in character. The National losses in these two days in killed, wounded and missing were not less than 14,000; those of the Confederates were almost as great. In this struggle General Alexander Hays was killed; Generals Getty, Baxter and McAlister were wounded, and scores of under-officers, with thousands of brave men, lost their lives or limbs. Now it was that Lee is reported to have said to his officers, with a serious look on his iron face: "Gentlemen, at last the Army of the Potomac has a head."

On the seventh of May there was not much fighting. It is said that in the lull Grant's leading commanders thought he would recede, as his predecessors had done, and that not a few of them gave it as their opinion that he should do so. It is said that when coming to the Chancellorsville House, he gave the command, "Forward, by the left flank," thus demonstrating his purpose, as he said four days afterward in his despatch to the government, "to fight it out on that line if it took all summer," the soldiers gave a sigh of relief, and many began to sing at the prospect of no more retreating. General Sherman has recorded his belief that at this juncture Grant best displayed his greatness.

With the movement which we have just mentioned, the next stage in the campaign would bring both the Union and the Confederate armies to Spottsylvania Courthouse. The distance that each had to march to that point was about the same. It was at this juncture that the woods in which the two armies were moving, Grant to the left and Lee to the right, took fire and were burned. When the Union advance came in sight of Spottsylvania, Warren, who commanded, found that the place had been already occupied by the vigilant enemy. Hancock did not arrive in time to make an immediate attack, and Longstreet's corps was able to get into position before the pressure of the Union advance could be felt.

At this juncture Sheridan, in command of the Federal cavalry, was cut loose from the Union army and sent whirling with irresistible speed and momentum entirely around the rear of the Confederate army, destroying railroads, cutting communication, burning trains and liberating prisoners, as far as the very suburbs of Richmond.

The main divisions of the Union army came into position before Spottsylvania. Hancock had the right wing, and upon his left rested Warren. Sedgwick's corps was next in order, while Burnside held the left. Just as the commanders were forming their lines and some men at a Union battery seemed to shrink from the Confederate sharpshooters, Sedgwick went forward to encourage them, saying, "Men, they couldn't hit an elephant at that distance." But the next instant he himself fell dead! His command of the Sixth Corps was transferred to General Wright.

It now remained for Hancock on the extreme right to attack the Confederate left. This was done by Barlow's division, but without success. This attack and repulse was the real beginning of the battle of Spottsylvania. The Confederates in front were strongly intrenched, but near the northernmost point of their works what was thought to be a weak point in the line was discovered. This point was what is known as a *salient.* The position, however, was in the thick woods, or was at any rate concealed by the woods and ravines in front.

As soon as the position was discovered and its nature known, a large part of Wright's corps was sent against it. The attack was successful. The line was carried, and about a thousand men captured in the assault. But the reinforcements were not up promptly, and the assailants were driven back. A second assault ended in the same way. This fighting was on the evening of the tenth of May. The battle continued into the night, and the event hung dubious.

On the eleventh there was a heavy rain, but during that day General Grant, who placed great confidence in General Hancock and his corps, moved that brilliant officer to the point of attack before the *salient.* With the early light on the morning of the twelfth, Hancock sprang forward to the assault. So sudden and powerful was the charge that one-half of the distance had been traversed before the enemy knew what was coming. Then the storm burst wildly. The yell arose from one side, and the cheer from the other. Hancock's men in great force and with invincible courage sprang upon the breast-works, clubbed their guns, or went over bayonet foremost. They were met on the other side in like manner. The melee that ensued was perhaps the most dreadful hand-to-hand conflict of the war. The impetus of the Union attack was irresistible. Great numbers were killed on both sides, and the Confederates were overpowered.

General Edward Johnson and his division of about four thousand men were captured in the angle. General Stuart was also taken. He and Hancock had been friends in their student days at West Point. The story goes that Hancock, recognizing his prisoner, said, "How are you, Stuart?" and offered his hand. The hot Confederate answered, "I am *General* Stuart of the Confederate army, and under the circumstances I decline to take your hand." Hancock answered, "Under any other circumstances I should not have offered it!"

But there was no time for bantering. The very earth round about was in the chaos of roaring battle. Hancock had taken twenty guns with their horses, and about thirty battle flags. It was a tremendous capture, if he could hold his ground. No officer of the Union army ever showed to better advantage. The world may well forgive the touch of vanity and bluster in the undaunted Hancock, as he sent this despatch to Grant: "I have used up Johnson and am going into Hill." He found, however, that he should have terrible work even to keep the gain that he had made.

Lee no sooner perceived what was done than he threw heavy masses upon the position to retake it from the captors. Hancock was now on the wrong side of the angle! The Confederates came on during the day in five successive charges, the like of which for valor was hardly ever witnessed. The contested ground was literally piled with dead. There was hand-to-hand fighting. Men bayoneted each other through the crevices of the logs that had been piled up for defences. The storm of battle swept back and forth until the salient gained that name of "Death Angle" by which it will ever be known. The place became then and there the bloodiest spot that ever was washed with human life in America. The bushes and trees round about were literally shot away. At one point an oak tree, more than eighteen inches in diameter, was completely eaten off at the man-level by the bullet storm that beat against it. That tree in its fall crushed several men of a South Carolina regiment who still stood and fought in the death harvest that was going on.

The counter assaults of the Confederates, however, were in vain. They inflicted terrible losses, and were themselves mowed down by thousands; but they could not and did not retake the angle. Hancock and his heroes could not be dislodged. The battle of Spottsylvania died away with the night into sullen and awful silence, which was broken only by the groans of thousands of wounded men who could not be recovered from the bloody earth on which they had fallen. The antagonists lay crouching like lions, only a lion's spring apart, and neither would suffer the other, even for the sake of their common American humanity, to recover his dead.

In the retrospect it seems marvelous that within the memories of men now living and not yet old, so awful a struggle as that of the Death Angle in the Wilderness could have taken place between men of the same race and language, born under the flag of the same Republic, and cherishing the same sentiments and traditions and hopes.

# APPOMATTOX

Appomattox was not a battle, but the end of battles. Fondly do we hope that never again shall Americans lift against Americans the avenging hand in such a strife! Here at a little court-house, twenty-five miles east of Lynchburg, on the ninth of April, 1865, the great tragedy of our civil war was brought to a happy end. Here General Robert E. Lee, with the broken fragments of his Army of Northern Virginia, was brought by the inexorable logic of war to the end of that career which he had so bravely followed through four years of battle, much of which had shown him to be one of the great commanders of the century.

The story of the downfall of the Confederacy has been many times repeated. It has entered into our literature, and is known by heart wherever the history of the war is read. Generally, however, this story has been told as if the narrator approached the event from the Union side. We have the pursuit of General Lee from Petersburg westward, almost to the spurs of the Alleghanies. We follow in the wake. We see the unwearied efforts of the victorious host to close around the retreating army which has so long been the bulwark of the Confederacy. We hear the summons to surrender, and the answer of "*Not yet*;" but within a day that answer is reversed, and the stern wills of Lee and his fellow-commanders yield to the inexorable law of the strongest.

Only recently, however, the story has been told with great spirit from the Confederate side, by General John B. Gordon, who was at that time at the right hand of his commander-in-chief, and who stood by him to the last hour. General Gordon's account of the final struggle of the Confederate army and of the surrender is so graphic, so full of spirit, so warmed with the animation and devotion of a great soldier, that we here repeat his account of

### THE DEATH STRUGGLE.

We always retreated in good order, though always under fire. As we retreated we would wheel and fire, or repel a rush, and then stagger on to the next hilltop, or vantage ground, where a new fight would be made. And so on through the entire day. At night my men had no rest. We marched through the night in order to get a little respite from fighting. All night long I would see my poor fellows hobbling along, prying wagons or artillery out of the mud, and supplementing the work of our broken-down horses. At dawn, though, they would be in line ready for battle, and they would fight with the steadiness and valor of the Old Guard.

This lasted until the night of the seventh of April. The retreat of Lee's army was lit up with the fire and flash of battle, in which my brave men moved about like demigods for five days and nights. Then we were sent to the front for a rest, and Longstreet was ordered to cover the retreating army. On the evening of the eighth, when I had reached the front, my scout George brought me two men in Confederate uniform, who, he said, he believed to be the enemy, as he had seen them counting our men as they filed past. I had the men brought to my campfire, and examined them. They made a plausible defence, but George was positive they were spies, and I ordered them searched. He failed to find anything, when I ordered him to examine their boots. In the bottom of one of the boots I found an order from General Grant to General Ord, telling him to move by forced marches toward Lynchburg and cut off General Lee's retreat. The men then confessed that they were spies, and belonged to General Sheridan. They stated that they knew that the penalty of their course was death, but asked that I should not kill them, as the war could only last a few days longer, anyhow. I kept them prisoners, and turned them over to General Sheridan after the surrender. I at once sent the information to General Lee, and a short time afterward received orders to go to his headquarters. That night was held Lee's last council of war. There were present General Lee, General Fitzhugh Lee, as head of the cavalry, and Pendleton, as chief of the artillery, and myself. General Longstreet was, I think, too busily engaged to attend.

General Lee then exhibited to us the correspondence he had had with General Grant that day, and asked our opinion of the situation. It seemed that surrender was inevitable. The only chance of escape was that I could cut a way for the army through the lines in front of me. General Lee asked me if I could do this. I replied that I did not know what forces were in front of me; that if General Ord had not arrived—as we thought then he had not—with his heavy masses of infantry, I could cut through. I guaranteed that my men would cut a way through all the cavalry that could be massed in front of them. The council finally dissolved with the understanding that the army should be surrendered if I discovered the next morning, after feeling the enemy's line, that the infantry had arrived in such force that I could not cut my way through.

My men were drawn up in the little town of Appomattox that night. I still had about four thousand men under me, as the army had been divided into two commands and given to General Longstreet and myself. Early on the morning of the ninth I prepared for the assault upon the enemy's line, and began the last fighting done in Virginia. My men rushed forward gamely and broke the line of the enemy and captured two pieces of artillery. I was still unable to tell what I was fighting; I did not know whether I was striking infantry or dismounted cavalry. I only know that my men were driving them back, and were getting further and further through. Just then I had a message from General Lee, telling me a flag of truce was in existence, leaving it to my discretion as to what course to pursue. My men were still pushing their way on. I sent at once to hear from General Longstreet, feeling that, if he was marching toward me, we might still cut through and carry the army forward. I learned that he was about two miles off, with his face just opposite from mine, fighting for his life. I thus saw that the case was hopeless. The further each of us drove the enemy the further we drifted apart, and the more exposed we left our wagon trains and artillery, which were parked between us. Every line either of us broke only opened the gap the wider. I saw plainly that the Federals would soon rush in between us, and then there would have been no army. I, therefore, determined to send a flag of truce. I called Colonel Peyton of my staff to me, and told him that I wanted him to carry a flag of truce forward. He replied:

"General, I have no flag of truce."

I told him to get one. He replied:

"General, we have no flag of truce in our command."

Then said I, "Get your handkerchief, put it on a stick, and go forward."

"I have no handkerchief, General,"

"Then borrow one and go forward with it."

He tried, and reported to me that there was no handkerchief in my staff.

"Then, Colonel, use your shirt."

"You see, General, that we all have on flannel shirts."

At last, I believe, we found a man who had a white shirt. He gave it to us, and I tore off the back and tail, and, tying this to a stick, Colonel Peyton went out toward the enemy's lines. I instructed him simply to say to General Sheridan that General Lee had written to me that a flag of truce had been sent from his and Grant's headquarters, and that he could act as he thought best on this information. In a few moments he came back with some one representing General Sheridan. This officer said:

"General Sheridan requested me to present his compliments to you, and to demand the unconditional surrender of your army."

"Major, you will please return my compliments to General Sheridan, and say that I will not surrender."

"But, General, he will annihilate you."

"I am perfectly well aware of my situation. I simply gave General Sheridan some information on which he may or may not desire to act."

He went back to his lines, and in a short time General Sheridan came forward on an immense horse, and attended by a very large staff. Just here an incident occurred that came near having a serious ending. As General Sheridan was approaching I noticed one of my sharpshooters drawing his rifle down upon him. I at once called to him: "Put down your gun, sir; this is a flag of truce." But he simply settled it to his shoulder and was drawing a bead on Sheridan, when I leaned forward and jerked his gun. He struggled with me, but I finally raised it. I then loosed it, and he started to aim again. I caught it again, when he turned his stern, white face, all broken with grief and streaming with tears, up to me, and said: "Well, General, then let him keep on his own side."

The fighting had continued up to this point. Indeed, after the flag of truce, a regiment of my men, who had been fighting their way through toward where we were, and who did not know of a flag of truce, fired into some of Sheridan's cavalry. This was speedily stopped, however. I showed General Sheridan General Lee's note, and he determined to await events. He dismounted, and I did the same. Then, for the first time, the men seemed to understand what it all meant, and then the poor fellows broke down. The men cried like children. Worn, starved and bleeding as they were, they would rather have died than have surrendered. At one word from me they would have hurled themselves on the enemy, and have cut their way through or have fallen to a man with their guns in their hands. But I could not permit it. The great drama had been played to its end. But men are seldom permitted to look upon such a scene as the one presented here. That these men should have wept at surrendering so unequal a fight, at being taken out of this constant carnage and storm, at being sent back to their families; that they should have wept at having their starved and wasted forms lifted out of the jaws of death and placed once more before their hearthstones, was an exhibition of fortitude and patriotism that might set an example for all time.

# SEDAN

BY VICTOR HUGO.

The Second Empire of the French was pounded to powder in a bowl. This is literal, not figurative. To attempt to describe Sedan after Victor Hugo has described it for all mankind were a work futile and foolish. To Hugo we concede the palm among all writers, ancient and modern, as a delineator of battle. His description of the battle of Waterloo will outlast the tumulus and the lion which French patriotism has reared on the square where the last of the Old Guard perished. His description, though not elaborate, is equally graphic and final. He was returning, in September, 1871, from his fourth exile. He had been in Belgium in banishment for about eighteen years. It is in the "History of a Crime" that he tells the story. He says that he was re-entering France by the Luxembourg frontier, and had fallen asleep in the coach. Suddenly the jolt of the train coming to a standstill awoke him. One of the passengers said: "What place is this?" Another answered "Sedan." With a shudder, Hugo looked around. He says that to his mind and vision, as he gazed out, the paradise was a tomb. Before substituting his words for our own, we note only that nearly thirteen months had elapsed since Louis Napoleon and his 90,000 men had here been brayed in a mortar. Hugo's description of the scene and the event continues as follows:

The valley was circular and hollow, like the bottom of a crater; the winding river resembled a serpent; the hills high, ranged one behind the other, surrounded this mysterious spot like a triple line of inexorable walls; once there, there is no means of exit. It reminded me of the amphitheatres. An indescribable, disquieting vegetation, which seemed to be an extension of the Black Forest, overran all the heights, and lost itself in the horizon like a huge impenetrable snare; the sun shone, the birds sang, carters passed by whistling; sheep, lambs and pigeons were scattered about; leaves quivered and rustled; the grass, a densely thick grass, was full of flowers. It was appalling.

I seemed to see waving over this valley the flashing of the avenging angel's sword.

This word "Sedan" had been like a veil abruptly torn aside. The landscape had become suddenly filled with tragedy. Those shapeless eyes which the bark of trees delineates on the trunks were gazing—at what? At something terrible and lost to view.

In truth, that was the place! And at the moment when I was passing by, thirteen months all but a few days had elapsed. That was the place where the monstrous enterprise of the second of December had burst asunder. A fearful shipwreck!

The gloomy pathways of Fate cannot be studied without profound anguish of heart.

On the thirty-first of August, 1870, an army was reassembled, and was, as it were, massed together under the walls of Sedan, in a place called the Givonne Valley. This army was a French army—twenty-nine brigades, fifteen divisions, four army corps—90,000 men. This army was in this place without anyone being able to divine the reason; without order, without an object, scattered about—a species of heap of men thrown down there as though with the view of being seized by some huge hand.

This army either did not entertain, or appeared not to entertain, for the moment any immediate uneasiness. They knew, or at least they thought they knew, that the enemy was a long way off. On calculating the stages at four leagues daily, it was three days' march distant. Nevertheless, toward evening the leaders took some wise strategic precautions; they protected the army, which rested in the rear on Sedan and the Meuse, by two battle fronts, one composed of the Seventh Corps, and extending from Floing to Givonne, the other composed of the Twelfth Corps, extending from Givonne to Bazeilles; a triangle of which the Meuse formed the hypothenuse. The Twelfth Corps, formed of the three divisions of Lacretelle, Lartigue and Wolff, ranged on the right, with the artillery between the brigades, formed a veritable barrier, having Bazeilles and Givonne at each end, and Digny in its centre; the two divisions of Petit and Lheritier massed in the rear upon two lines supported this barrier. General Lebrun commanded the Twelfth Corps. The Seventh Corps, commanded by General Douay, only possessed two divisions—Dumont's division and Gilbert's division—and formed the other battle front, covering the army of Givonne to Floing on the side of Illy; this battle front was comparatively weak, too open on the side of Givonne, and only protected on the side of the Meuse by two cavalry divisions of Margueritte and Bonnemains, and by Guyomar's brigade, resting in squares on Floing. Within this triangle were encamped the Fifth Corps, commanded by General Wimpfen, and the First Corps, commanded by General Ducrot. Michel's cavalry division covered the First Corps on the side of Digny; the Fifth supported itself upon Sedan. Four divisions, each disposed upon two lines—the divisions of Lheritier, Grandchamp, Goze and Conseil-Dumenil—formed a sort of horseshoe, turned toward Sedan, and uniting the first battle front with the second. The cavalry division of Ameil and the brigade of Fontanges served as a reserve for these four divisions. The whole of the artillery was upon the two battle fronts. Two portions of the army were in confusion, one to the right of Sedan beyond Balan, the other to the left of Sedan, on this side of Iges. Beyond Balan were the division of Vassoigne and the brigade of Reboul, on this side of Iges were the two cavalry divisions of Margueritte and Bonnemains.

These arrangements indicated a profound feeling of security. In the first place, the Emperor Napoleon III. would not have come there if he had not been perfectly tranquil. This Givonne Valley is what Napoleon I. called a "wash-hand basin." There could not have been a more complete enclosure. An army is so much at home there that it is too much so; it runs the risk of no longer being able to get out. This disquieted some brave and prudent leaders, such as Wimpfen, but they were not listened to. If absolutely necessary, said the people of the imperial circle, they could always be sure of being able to reach Mezieres, and at the worst the Belgian frontier. Was it, however, needful to provide for such extreme eventualities? In certain cases foresight is almost an offence. They were all of one mind, therefore, to be at their ease.

If they had been uneasy they would have cut the bridges of the Meuse, but they did not even think of it. To what purpose? The enemy was a long way off. The Emperor, who evidently was well informed, affirmed it.

The army bivouacked somewhat in confusion, as we have said, and slept peaceably throughout this night of August 31, having, whatever might happen, or believing that they had, the retreat upon Mezieres open behind it. They disdained to take the most ordinary precautions, they made no cavalry reconnoissances, they did not even place outposts. A German military writer has stated this. Fourteen leagues at least separated them from the German army, three days' march; they did not exactly know where it was; they believed it scattered, possessing little unity, badly informed, led somewhat at random upon several points at once, incapable of a movement converging upon one single point, like Sedan; they believed that the Crown Prince of Saxony was marching on Chalons, and that the Crown Prince of Prussia was marching on Metz; they were ignorant of everything appertaining to this army, its leaders, its plan, its armament, its effective force. Was it still following the strategy of Gustavus Adolphus? Was it still following the tactics of Frederick II.? No one knew. They felt sure of being at Berlin in a few weeks. What nonsense! The Prussian army! They talked of this war as of a dream, and of this army as of a phantom....

The masterful description of the great novelist and poet then continues in a narrative of the attack and catastrophe:

Bazeilles takes fire, Givonne takes fire, Floing takes fire; the battle begins with a furnace. The whole horizon is aflame. The French camp is in this crater, stupefied, affrighted, starting up from sleeping—a funereal swarming. A circle of thunder surrounds the army. They are encircled by annihilation. This mighty slaughter is carried on on all sides simultaneously. The French resist and they are terrible, having nothing left but despair. Our cannon, almost all old-fashioned and of short range, are at once dismounted by the fearful and exact aim of the Prussians. The density of the rain of shells upon the valley is so great that "the earth is completely furrowed," says an eye-witness, "as though by a rake." How many cannon? Eleven hundred at least. Twelve German batteries upon La Moncelle alone; the Third and Fourth *Abtheilung*, an awe-striking artillery, upon the crests of Givonne, with the Second Horse Battery in reserve; opposite Digny ten Saxon and two Wurtemburg batteries; the curtain of trees of the wood to the north of Villers-Cernay masks the mounted *Abtheilung*, which is there with the third Heavy Artillery in reserve, and from the gloomy copse issues a formidable fire; the twenty-four pieces of the First Heavy Artillery are ranged in the glade skirting the road from La Moncelle to La Chapelle; the battery of the Royal Guard sets fire to the Garenne Wood; the shells and the balls riddle Suchy, Francheval, Fouro-Saint-Remy, and the valley between Heibes and Givonne; and the third and fourth rank of cannon extend without break of continuity as far as the Calvary of Illy, the extreme point of the horizon. The German soldiers, seated or lying before the batteries, watch the artillery at work. The French soldiers fall and die. Amongst the bodies which cover the plain there is one, the body of an officer, on which they will find, after the battle, a sealed note containing this order, signed Napoleon: "To-day, September 1, rest for the whole army."

The gallant Thirty-fifth of the Line almost entirely disappears under the overwhelming shower of shells; the brave Marine Infantry holds at bay for a moment the Saxons, joined by the Bavarians, but outflanked on every side draws back; all the admirable cavalry of the Margueritte division hurled against the German infantry halts and sinks down midway, "annihilated," says the Prussian report, "by well-aimed and cool firing." This field of carnage has three outlets, all three barred: the Bouillon road by the Prussian Guard, the Carignan road by the Bavarians, the Mezieres road by the Wurtemburgers. The French have not thought of barricading the railway viaduct; three German battalions have occupied it during the night. Two isolated houses on the Balan road could be made the pivot of a long resistance, but the Germans are there. The wood from Monvilliers to Bazeilles, but the French have been forestalled; they find the Bavarians cutting the underwood with their billhooks. The German army moves in one piece, in one absolute unity; the Crown Prince of Saxony is on the height of Mairy, whence he surveys the whole action; the command oscillates in the French army; at the beginning of the battle, at a quarter to six, MacMahon is wounded by the bursting of a shell; at seven o'clock Ducrot replaces him; at ten o'clock Wimpfen replaces Ducrot. Every instant the wall of fire is drawing closer in, the roll of the thunder is continuous, a dismal pulverization of 90,000 men! Never before has anything equal to this been seen; never before has an army been overwhelmed beneath such a downpour of lead and iron! At one o'clock all is lost! The regiments fly helter-skelter into Sedan! But Sedan begins to burn, Dijonval burns, the ambulances burn, there is nothing now possible but to cut their way out. Wimpfen, brave and resolute, proposes this to the Emperor. The Third Zouaves, desperate, have set the example. Cut off from the rest of the army, they have forced a passage and have reached Belgium. A flight of lions!

Suddenly, above the disaster, above the huge pile of dead and dying, above all this unfortunate heroism, appears disgrace. The white flag is hoisted.

# BAZAINE AND METZ

A letter of Count Von Moltke has recently been published, showing that the question of the conquest of France was under consideration by the Count and Bismarck as early as August of 1866. It is demonstrated that these two powerful spirits were already preparing, aye, had already prepared, to trip the Emperor Louis Napoleon, throwing him and his Empire into a common ruin. The letter also proves that the plan of the North-German Confederation, under the leadership of Prussia, with German unity and a German Empire just beyond, was already clearly in mind by the far-sighted leaders who surrounded King William in 1866. Count Von Moltke shows that it was possible and practicable *at that date*, and within a period of two or three weeks, to throw upon the French border so tremendous an army that resistance would be impossible. The antecedents of the Franco-Prussian War had been clearly thought out by the German masters at a time when Louis Napoleon was still tinkering with his quixotical Empire in Mexico.

When the war between France and Germany actually broke out, four years later. Germany was prepared, and France was unprepared for the conflict. Louis Napoleon did not know that Germany was prepared. He actually thought that he could break into the German borders, fight his way victoriously to the capital, make his headquarters in Berlin, and dictate a peace in the manner of his uncle. It was the most fallacious dream that a really astute man ever indulged in. From the first day of actual contact with the Germans, the dream of the Emperor began to be dissipated. Within five days (August 14-18, 1870,) three murderous battles were fought on French soil, the first at Courcelles, the next at Vionville, and the third at Gravelotte. In all of these the French fought bravely, and in all were defeated disastrously, with tremendous losses.

By these great victories, the Germans were able to separate the two divisions of the French army. The northern division, under command of the Emperor and MacMahon, began to recede toward Sedan, while the more powerful army, under Marshal Bazaine, numbering 173,000 men, was forced somewhat to the south, and pressed by the division of Prince Frederick Charles, until the French, in an evil day, entered the fortified town of Metz, and suffered themselves to be helplessly cooped up. There was perhaps never another great army so safely and hopelessly disposed of!

Metz, after Antwerp, is the strongest fortress in Europe. It is situated at the junction of the rivers Seille and Moselle. It is the capital of the province of Lorraine, destined to be lost by France and gained by Germany in the struggle that was now on. The place was of great historical importance. Here the Roman invaders had established themselves in the time of the conquest of Gaul. It was called by the conquerors, first Mediomatrica, and afterward Divodurum. Its importance, on the very crest of the watershed between the Teutonic and Gallic races, was noted in the early years of our era, and to the present day that importance continues for the same reason as of old. Metz is on the line of a conflict of races which has not yet, after so many centuries, been finally decided.

The position is one of great strategic importance. But such were the military conditions at the end of August, 1870, that to occupy Metz with one of the greatest armies of modern times was the most serious disaster that could befall the French cause. Bazaine's army was needed, not in a fortified town, but *in the field.* It was a tremendous force. The army that Prince Frederick Charles locked up in Metz could have marched from Parthia to Spain against the resistance of the whole Roman Empire, at the high noon of that imperial power! It could have marched from end to end of the Southern Confederacy in the palmiest day of that Confederacy, and could not have been seriously impeded! And yet this tremendous force was pent up and shut in, as if under seal, while King William and the Crown Prince and Bismarck and Von Moltke hunted down the French Emperor and his remaining forces, brought them to bay, and compelled a surrender.

This was accomplished by the first of September. The Empire of Napoleon went to pieces. The Third Republic was instituted. The Empress fled with the Prince Imperial to England, while her humbled lord was established by his captors at the castle of Wilhelmshohe. Republican France found herself in possession of a political chaos which could hardly be stilled. She also found herself in possession of a splendid army of more than one hundred and seventy thousand men shut up helplessly in Metz. The situation was highly dramatic. The Republic said that Bazaine should break out, but the Marshal said that he could not. What he said was true. The Germans held him fast. But the Republic believed, as it still believes, that Bazaine, loyal to the fallen Emperor rather than to his country, wished to handle his army in such a manner as should compel the restoration of the Empire, under the auspices of the German conquerors.

This idea was hateful above all things to the French Republicans. September wore away, and more than half of October; but still the siege of Metz was not concluded. Vainly did the new Republic of France strive to extricate herself. Vainly did she raise new armies. Vainly did she look for the escape of Bazaine. Finally, on the twenty-seventh of October, that commander surrendered Metz and his army to the Germans. It was the most tremendous capitulation known in history. Never before was so powerful an army surrendered to an enemy. The actual number of French soldiers covered by the capitulation was fully one hundred and seventy thousand! The prostration of France was complete, and her humiliation extreme.

Bazaine became the Black Beast of the public imagination. A tribunal was organized at Paris, under the presidency of the Duc d'Aumale, son of Louis Philippe—the same who with the Prince de Joinville had been on McClellan's staff during the peninsular campaign in our Civil War. Before this court Bazaine was haled as a traitor to his country. He was tried, convicted and condemned to degradation and death. It was only by the most strenuous efforts in his behalf that a commutation of the sentence to imprisonment for twenty years was obtained.

The Marshal was accordingly incarcerated in a prison at Cannes, whither he was sent in December of 1873, and from which he effected his escape in the following August. He succeeded in making his way to Madrid, and took up his residence there. He sought assiduously by writings and argument and appeal to reverse the judgment of his countrymen and of the world with regard to the justice of his sentence; but he could not succeed. It is probably true that the greatest surrender of military forces known in the history of the world was brought about by the preference of the commanding general of the conquered army for an Emperor who was already dethroned, as against a true devotion to his country. There was also in the case a measure of incapacity. Bazaine was no match as a military commander for the powerful genius of Von Moltke and the persistency of Frederick Charles and the more than two hundred thousand resolute Germans who surrounded him, and brought him and his army to irretrievable ruin.

---

# Astronomical Vistas

# THE CENTURY OF ASTEROIDS

The nineteenth century may be called the Age of the Asteroids. It was on *the first night* of this century that the first asteroid was discovered! Through all the former ages, no man on the earth had had definite knowledge of the existence of such a body. It was reserved for Guiseppe Piazzi, an Italian astronomer at Palermo, to make known by actual observation the first member of the planetoid group. If human history had the slightest regard for the calendars of mankind—if the eternal verities depended in any measure on the almanac or the division of time into this age or that—we might look with wonder on the remarkable coincidence which made the discovery of the first asteroid to happen in the first evening twilight of the first day of the nineteenth century!

At the close of the eighteenth century, mankind were acquainted with all the major planets except Neptune. Uranus, the last of the group, was discovered by the Elder Herschel, on the night of the thirteenth of March, 1781. True, this planet had been seen on twenty different occasions, by other observers; but its character had not been revealed. Sir William called his new world Georgium Sidus, that is, the George Star, in honor of the King of England. The world, however, had too much intelligence to allow the transfer of the name of George III. from earth to heaven. Such nomenclature would have been unpopular in America! The name of the king was happily destined to remain a part of terrestrial history!

For a while it was insisted by astronomers and the world at large that the new globe, then supposed to bound the solar system on its outer circumference, should be called Herschel, in honor of its discoverer. But the old system of naming the planets after the deities of classical and pagan mythology prevailed; and to the names of Mercury, Venus, Mars, Jupiter, Saturn, was now added the name Uranus, that is, in the language of the Greeks, *Heaven.*

Piazzi, scanning the zodiac from his observatory in Palermo, in the early hours of that first night of the century, noticed a hitherto unobserved star, which under higher power proved to be a planet. It presented a small irregular disc, and a few additional observations showed that it was progressing in the usual manner from west to east. For some time such a revelation had been expected; but the result did not answer to expectation in one particular; for the new body seemed to be too insignificant to be called a world. It appeared rather to be a great planetary boulder, as if our Mount Shasta had been wrenched from the earth and flung into space.

Investigation showed that the new body was more than a hundred miles in diameter; but this, according to planetary estimation, is only the measurement of a clod.

There had been, as we say, expectation of a discovery in the region where the first asteroid was found. Kepler had declared his belief that in this region of space a new world might be discovered. Following this suggestion, the German astronomer Olbers, of Bremen, had formed an association of twenty-four observers in different parts of Europe, who should divide among themselves the zodiacal band, and begin a system of independent scrutiny, either to verify or disprove Kepler's hypothesis.

There was another reason also of no small influence tending to the same end. Johann Elert Bode, another German astronomer, born in 1747 and living to 1826, had propounded a mathematical formula known as Bode's Law, which led those who accepted it to the belief that a planet would be found in what is now known as the asteroidal space. Bode's Law, so-called, seems to be no real law of planetary distribution; and yet the coincidences which are found under the application of the law are such as to arouse our interest if not to produce a conviction of the truth of the principle involved. Here, then, is the mathematical formula, which is known as Bode's Law:

Write from left to right a row of 4's and under these, beginning with the second 4, place a geometrical series beginning with 3 and increasing by the ratio of 2; add the two columns together, and we have a series running 4, 7, 10, etc.; and this row of results has an astonishing coincidence, or approximate coincidence with the relative distances of the planets from the sun—thus:

| | | | | | | | | |
|---|---|---|---|---|---|---|---|---|
| 4 | 4 | 4 | 4 | 4 | 4 | 4 | 4 | 4 |
| | 3 | 6 | 12 | 24 | 48 | 96 | 192 | 384 |
| -- | -- | -- | -- | -- | -- | --- | --- | --- |
| 4 | 7 | 10 | 16 | 28 | 52 | 100 | 196 | 388 |

The near agreement of this row of results with the row containing the *actual* relative distances of the planets from the sun may well astonish, not only the astronomer, but the common reader. Those distances—making 10 to represent the distance of the earth—are as follows:

Mercury, 3.9; Venus, 7.2; Earth, 10; Mars, 15.2; Asteroids, 27.4; Jupiter, 52; Saturn, 95.4; Uranus, 192; Neptune, 300.

In addition to Kepler's prediction and the indications of Bode's Law, there was a *general* reason for thinking that a planetary body of some kind should occupy the space between the orbits of Mars and Jupiter. The mean distance of Mars from the sun is about 141,500,000 miles; that of Jupiter, is about 483,000,000 miles. The distance from one orbit to the other is therefore about 341,500,000 miles. Conceive of an infinite sheet of tin. Mark thereon a centre for the sun. Measure out a hundred and forty millions of miles, and with that radius strike a circle. From the same centre measure out four hundred and eighty-three millions of miles, and with that radius strike a circle. Cut out the sheet between the two circles, and the vast space left void will indicate the vacant area in the mighty disc of our solar system. That this space should be occupied with *something* accords with the plan of nature and the skill of the Builder.

So Olbers and his twenty-three associates began, in the last decade of the eighteenth century, to search diligently for the verification of Kepler's prediction and the fulfillment of Bode's Law. Oddly enough, Piazzi was not one of the twenty-four astronomers who had agreed to find the new world. He was exploring the heavens on his own account, and in doing so, he found what the others had failed to find, that is, the first asteroid.

The body discovered answered so little to the hopes of the astronomical fraternity that they immediately said within themselves: "This is not he; we seek another." So they continued the search, and in a little more than a year Olbers himself was rewarded with the discovery of the second of the planetoid group. On the twenty-eighth of March, 1802, he made his discovery from an upper chamber of his dwelling in Bremen, where he had his telescope. On the night in question he was scanning the northern part of the constellation of Virgo, when the sought-for object was found. This body, like the first of its kind, was very small, and was found to be moving from west to east in nearly the same orbit as its predecessor.

Here then was something wonderful. Olbers at once advanced the hypothesis that probably the two bodies thus discovered were fragments of what had been a large planet moving in its orbit through this part of the heavens. If so there might be—and probably were—others of like kind. The search was at once renewed, and on the night of the first of September, 1804, the third of the asteroid group was found by the astronomer Hardy, of Bremen. The belief that a large planet had been disrupted in this region was strengthened, and astronomers continued their exploration; but two years and a half elapsed before another asteroid was found. On the evening of March 29, 1807, the diligence of Olbers was rewarded with the discovery of the fourth of the group, which like its predecessors, was so small and irregular in character as still further to favor the fragmentary theory.

How shall we name the asteroids? Piazzi fell back upon pagan mythology for the name of his little world, and called it Ceres, from the Roman goddess of corn. Olbers named the second asteroid Pallas; the third was called Juno—whose rank in the Greek and Roman pantheon might have suggested one of the major planets as her representative in the skies; and the fourth was called Vesta, from the Roman divinity of the hearthstone.

Here then there was a pause. Though the zodiac continued to be swept by many observers, a period of more than thirty-eight years went by before the fifth asteroid was found. The cycle of these discoveries strikingly illustrates the general movement of scientific progress. First there is a new departure; then a lull, and then a resumption of exploration and a finding more fertile than ever. It was on the night of the eighth of December, 1845, that the German astronomer Hencke discovered the fifth asteroid and named it Astræa. After a year and a half, namely, on the night of the first of July, 1847, the same observer discovered the sixth member of the group, and to this was given the name Hebe. On the thirteenth of August in the same year the astronomer Hind found the seventh asteroid, and named it Iris. On the eighteenth of October following he found the eighth, and this was called Flora. Then on the twenty-fifth of April, 1848, came the discovery of Metis, by Graham. Nearly a year later the Italian De Gasparis found the tenth member of the system, that is, Hygeia. De Gasparis soon discovered the eleventh body, which was called Parthenope. This was on the eleventh of May, 1850.

Two other asteroids were found in this year; and two in 1851. In the following year *nine* were discovered; and so on from year to year down to the present date. Some years have been fruitful in such finds, while others have been comparatively barren. In a number of the years, only a single asteroid has been added to the list; but in others whole groups have been found. Thus in 1861 twelve were discovered; in 1868, twelve; in 1875, *seventeen*; in 1890, fourteen. Not a single year since 1846 has passed without the addition of at least one known asteroid to the list.

But while the number has thus increased to an aggregate at the close of 1890 of three hundred and one, many of the tiny wanderers have escaped. Some have been rediscovered; and it is possible that some have been twice or even three times found and named. The whole family perhaps numbers not only hundreds, but thousands; and it can hardly be doubted that only the more conspicuous members of the group have ever yet been seen by mortal eye.

A considerable space about the centre of the planetary zone between Mars and Jupiter is occupied with these multitudinous pigmy worlds that follow the one the other in endless flight around the sun. It is a sort of planetary shower; and it can hardly be doubted that the bodies constituting the flight are graded down in size from larger to smaller and still smaller until the fragments are mere blocks and bits of world-dust floating in space. Possibly there may be enough of such matter to constitute a sort of planetary band that may illumine a little (as seen from a distance) the zone where it circulates.

As to the origin of this seemingly fragmentary matter, we know nothing, and conjectures are of little use in scientific exposition. It may be true that a large planet once occupied the asteroidal space, and that the same has been rent by some violence into thousands of fragments. It may be observed that the period of rotation of the inferior planets corresponds in general with that of our earth, while the corresponding period of the superior or outside planets is less than one-half as great. The forces which produced this difference in the period of rotation may have contended for the mastery in that part of our solar system where the asteroids are found; and the disruption may have resulted from such conflict of forces.

Or again, it may be that a large planet is now in process of formation in the asteroidal space. Possibly one of the greater fragments may gain in mass by attracting to itself the nearer fragments, and thus continue to wax until it shall have swept clean the whole pathway of the planetary matter, except such small fragments as may after æons of time continue to fall upon the master body, as our meteorites now at intervals rush into our atmosphere and sometimes reach the earth.

Some astronomers have given and are still giving their almost undivided attention to asteroidal investigation. The discoveries have been mostly made by a few principal explorers. The astronomer, Palisa, from the observatory of Pola and that of Vienna, has found no fewer than seventy-five of the whole group. The observer, Peters, at Clinton, New York, has found forty-eight asteroids; Luther, of Düsseldorf, twenty-four; Watson, of Ann Arbor, twenty-two; Borrelly, of Marseilles, fifteen; Goldschmidt, of Paris, fourteen, and Charlois, of Nice, fourteen. The English astronomers have found only a few. Among such, Hind of London, who has-discovered ten asteroids, is the leader.

The Italian, German and American astronomers are first in the interest and success which they have shown in this branch of sky-lore. Their investigations have made us acquainted with the dim group of little worlds performing their unknown part in the vast space between the Warrior planet and Jove.

# THE STORY OF NEPTUNE

The discovery of the planet Neptune by Dr. Galle on the twenty-third of September, 1846, was one of the most important events in the intellectual history of this century. Certainly it was no small thing to find a new world. Discoverers on the surface of our globe are immortalized by finding new lands in unknown regions. What, therefore, should be the fame of him who finds a new world in the depths of space? Perhaps the discoverer of an asteroid or planetary moon may not claim, in the present advanced stage of human knowledge, to rank among the flying evangels of history; but he who found the great planet third in rank among the worlds of the solar system, a world having a mass nearly seventeen times as great as that of our own, may well be regarded as one of the immortals.

We have referred the discovery of Neptune to Dr. Johann Gottfried Galle, the German astronomer and Professor of Natural Sciences at Berlin. But this Dr. Galle was only the *eye* with which the discovery was made. He was a good eye; but the eye, however clear, is only an organ of something greater than the eye, and that something in this case consisted of two parts. The first part was Urbain Jean Joseph Leverrier, the French astronomer, of the Paris Observatory. The other part was Professor John Couch Adams, the astronomer of the University at Cambridge, England. These two were the thinkers; that is, they were, as it were, jointly the great mind of the age, of which Galle was the eye.

In getting a clear notion of the discovery of Neptune, several other personages are to be considered. One of these is the astronomer Alexis Bouvart, of France, who was born in Haute Savoie, in 1767, and died in June of 1843, three years before Neptune was found. Another personage was his nephew, the astronomer E. Bouvart, and a third was the noted Prussian, Friedrich Wilhelm Bessel, Director of the Observatory at Königsberg, who was born in 1784, and died on the seventeenth of March, 1846, only six months before the discovery of our outer planet.

Still another character to be commemorated is the English astronomer Professor James Challis, Plumian Professor and Director of the Observatory at Cambridge, England. This contributor to the great event was born in 1803, and died at Cambridge on the third of December, 1882. Still another, not to be disregarded, is Dr. T.J. Hussey, of Hayes, England, whose mind seems to have been one of the first to anticipate the existence of an ultra-Uranian planet. And still again, the English astronomer royal, Sir G.B. Airy must be mentioned as a contributor to the final result; but he is to be regarded rather as a contributor by negation. The great actors in the thing done were Leverrier, Adams and Galle. English authors contend strongly for placing the names in this order: Adams, Leverrier and Galle.

Suffice it to say that when Uranus was discovered by the elder Herschel in 1781, that world was supposed to be the outside planet of our system. Hitherto the splendid Saturn had marked the uttermost excursion of astronomical knowledge as it respected our solar group. For about a quarter of a century after Herschel's discovery the world rested upon it as a finality. The orbit of Uranus was thought to circumscribe the whole. But in the meantime, observations of this orbit led to the knowledge that it did not conform in all respects to astronomical and mathematical conditions. The orbit showed irregularities, disturbances, perturbations, that could not be accounted for when all of the known mathematical calculations were applied thereto. Uranus was seen to get out of his path. At times he would lag a little, and then at other times appear to be accelerated. Each year, when the earth would swing around on the Uranian side of the sun, the observations were renewed, but always with the result that the planet did not seem to conform perfectly to the conditions of his orbit. What could be the cause of this seeming disregard of mathematical laws?

Astronomers could not accept the supposition that there was any actual violation of the known conditions of gravitation. Certainly Uranus was following his orbit under the centripetal and centrifugal laws in the same manner as the other planets. There must, therefore, be some undiscovered disturbing cause. It had already been noted that in the case of the infra-Uranian planets they were swayed somewhat from their paths by the mutual influence of one upon the other. This was noticeable in particular in the movements of Jupiter, Saturn and Uranus. When Saturn, for instance, would be on the same side of the sun with Jupiter, it might be noted that the latter was drawn outward and the former inward from their prescribed curves. The perturbation was greatest when the planets were nearest, together. In like manner Uranus did obeisance to both his huge neighbors on the sun's side of his orbit. He, too, veered toward them as he passed, and they in turn recognized the courtesy by going out of their orbits as they passed. What, therefore, should be said of the outswinging movement of Uranus from his orbit in that part of his course where no disturbing influence was known to exist? Certainly *something* must be in that quarter of space to occasion the perturbation. What was it?

It would appear that the elder Bouvart, the French astronomer referred to above, was the first to suggest that the disturbances in the orbit of Uranus, throwing that planet from his pathway outward, might be and probably were to be explained by the presence in outer space of an unknown ultra-Uranian planet. Bouvart prepared tables to show the perturbations in question, and declared his opinion that they were caused by an unknown planet beyond. No observer, however, undertook to verify this suggestion or to disprove it. Nor did Bouvart go so far as to indicate the particular part of the heavens which should be explored in order to find the undiscovered world. His tables, however, do show from the perturbations of the orbits of Jupiter, Saturn and Uranus that the same are caused by the mutual influence of the planets upon one another.

It seems to have remained for Dr. T.J. Hussey, of Hayes, England, to suggest the actual discovery of the unknown planet by following the clew of the disturbance produced by its presence in a certain field of space. Dr. Hussey, in 1834, wrote to Sir George Biddell Airy, astronomer royal at Greenwich, suggesting that the perturbation of the orbit of Uranus might be used as the clew for the discovery of the planet beyond. But Sir George was one of those safe, conservative scholars who scorn to follow the suggestions of genius, preferring rather to explore only what is known already. He said in answer that he doubted if the irregularity in the Uranian orbit was in such a state of demonstration as to give any hope of the discovery of the disturbing cause. He doubted even that there was such irregularity in the Uranian orbit. He was of opinion that the observers had been mistaken in the alleged detection of perturbations. So the Greenwich observatory was not used on the line of exploration suggested by Hussey.

Three years afterward, and again in 1842, Sir George received letters from the younger Bouvart, again suggesting the possibility and probability of discovering the ultra-Uranian planet. These hints were strengthened by a letter from Bessel, of Königsberg. But Sir George B. Airy refused to be led in the direction of so great a possibility.

It was in 1844 that Professor James Challis, of the Cambridge observatory, appealed to Sir George for the privilege of using or examining the recorded observations made at Greenwich of the movements of Uranus, saying that he wished these tables for a young friend of his, Mr. John C. Adams, of Cambridge, who had but recently taken his degree in mathematics. Adams was at that date only twenty-five years of age. The royal astronomer granted the request, and for about a year Adams was engaged in making his calculations. These were completed, and in September of 1845, Challis informed Sir George Airy that according to the calculations of Adams the perturbations of Uranus were due to the influence of an unknown planet beyond.

The young mathematician indicated in his conclusions at what point in the heavens the ultra-Uranian world was then traveling, and where it might be found. But even these mathematical demonstrations did not suffice to influence Sir George in his opinions. He was an Englishman! He refused or neglected to take the necessary steps either to verify or to disprove the conclusions of Adams. He held in hand the mathematical computations of that genius from October of 1845 to June of the following year, when the astronomer Leverrier, of Paris, published to the world his own tables of computation, proving that the disturbances in the orbit of Uranus were due to the influence of a planet beyond, and indicating the place where it might be found. There was a close agreement between the point indicated by him and that already designated by Adams.

It seems that this French publication at last aroused Sir George Airy, who now admitted that the calculations of Adams might be correct in form and deduction. He accordingly sent word to Professor Challis to begin a search for the unknown orb. The latter did begin the work of exploration, and presently saw the planet. But he failed to recognize it! There it was; but the observer passed it over as a fixed star. As for Leverrier, he sent his calculations to Dr. Galle, of Berlin; and that great observer began his search. On the night of the twenty-third of September, 1846, he not only *saw* but *caught* the far-off world. There it was, disc and all; and a few additional observations confirmed the discovery.

Hereupon Sir George Airy broke out with a claim that the discovery belonged to Adams. He was able to show that Adams had anticipated Leverrier by a few months in his calculations; but the French scholars were able to carry the day by showing that Adams' work had been void of results. The world went with the French claim. Adams was left to enjoy the fame of merit among the learned classes, but the great public fixed upon Leverrier as the genius who did the work, and Dr. Galle as his eye.

Several remarkable things followed in the train. It was soon discovered that both Leverrier and Adams had been favored by chance in indicating the field of space where Uranus was found. They had both proceeded upon the principle expressed in Bode's Law. This law indicated the place of Neptune as 38.8 times the distance of the earth from the sun. A verification of the result showed that the new-found planet was actually only thirty times as far as the earth from the sun. In the case of all the other planets, their distances had been remarkably co-incident with the results reached by Bode's Law; but Uranus seemed to break that law, or at least to bend it to the point of breaking—a result which has never to this day been explained.

It chanced, however, that at the time when the predictions of Leverrier and Adams were sent, the one sent to Galle and the other to Challis, Uranus and the earth and the sun were in such relations that the departure of the orbit of Uranus from the place indicated by Bode's Law did not seriously displace the planet from the position which it should theoretically occupy. Thus, after a little searching, Challis found the new world, and knew it not; Galle found it and knew it, and tethered it to the planetary system, making it fast in the recorded knowledge of mankind.

While Daniel O'Connell, the greatest Irishman of the present century, despairing of the cause of his country, lay dying in Genoa, and while Zachary Taylor, at the head of a handful of American soldiers was cooping up the Mexican army in the old town of Monterey, a new world, 37,000 miles in diameter and seventeen times as great in mass as the little world on which we dwell, was found slowly and sublimely making its way around the well nigh inconceivable periphery of the solar system!

# EVOLUTION OF THE TELESCOPE

The development of telescopic power within the present century is one of the most striking examples of intellectual progress and mastery in the history of mankind. The first day of the century found us, not, indeed, where we were left by Galileo and Copernicus in the knowledge of the skies and in our ability to penetrate their depths, but it did find us advanced by only moderate stages from the sky-lore of the past.

The after half of the eighteenth century presents a history of astronomical investigation and deduction which confirmed and amplified the preceding knowledge; but that period did not greatly widen the field of observation. If the sphere of space which had been explored on the first day of January, 1801, could be compared with that which is now known and explored by our astronomers, the one sphere would be to the other even as an apple to the earth.

It is difficult to apprehend the tremendous strides which we have made in the production of telescopes and the consequent increase in our sweep of the heavens. It was only in 1774 that the elder Herschel began his work in the construction of reflecting telescopes. These he gradually increased in size, until near the close of the century, when he produced an instrument which magnified two hundred and twenty-seven diameters. In the course of his career he built two hundred telescopes, having a seven-foot focus; 150 of ten feet and about eighty of twenty feet each.

With these instruments the astronomical work in the last quarter of the eighteenth century was mostly performed. The study of the heavens at this epoch began to reach out from the planetary system to the fixed stars. In this work Herschel led the way. The planet Uranus at first bore the name of Herschel, from its discoverer. Sir John Herschel, son of Sir William, was born in 1792. All of his astronomical work was accomplished in our century. Following the line of his father, he used the reflecting telescope, and it was an instrument of this kind that he took to his observatory at the Cape of Good Hope. Lord Rosse was born in the year 1800. Under his auspices the reflecting telescope reached its maximum of power and usefulness. His great reflector, built in his own grounds at Birr Castle, Ireland, was finished in 1844. This instrument was the marvel of that epoch. It had a focal distance of fifty-three feet, and an aperture of six feet. With this great telescope its master reached out into the region of the nebulæ, and began the real work of exploring the sidereal heavens.

In the reflecting telescope, however, there are necessary limitations. Before the middle of this century, it was known that the future of astronomy depended upon the refracting lens, and not on the speculum. The latter, in the hands of the two Herschels and Rosse, had reached its utmost limits—as is shown by the fact that to this day the Rosse telescope is the largest of its kind in the world.

Meanwhile the production of refracting telescopes made but slow progress. As late as 1836 the largest instrument of this kind in the world was the eleven-inch telescope of the observatory at Munich. The next in importance was a nine and a half-inch instrument at Dorpat, in Russia. This was the telescope through which the astronomer Struve made his earlier studies and discoveries. His field of observation was for the most part the fixed and double stars. At this time the largest instrument in the United States was the five-inch refractor of Yale College. Soon afterward, namely, in 1840, the observatory at Philadelphia was supplied with a six-inch refracting telescope from Munich.

German makers were now in the lead, and it was not long until a Munich instrument having a lens of eleven inches diameter was imported for the Mitchell Observatory on Mount Adams, overlooking Cincinnati. About the same time a similar instrument of nine and a half inches aperture was imported for the National Observatory at Washington. To this period also belongs the construction of the Cambridge Observatory, with its fifteen-inch refracting telescope. Another of the same size was produced for the Royal Observatory at Pulkova, Russia. This was in 1839; and that instrument and the telescope at Cambridge were then the largest of their kind in the world.

The history of the telescope-making in America properly begins with Alvan Clark, Sr., of Cambridgeport, Massachusetts. It was in 1846 that he produced his first telescope. Of this he made the lens, and such was the excellence of his work that he soon became famous, to the degree that the importation of foreign telescopes virtually ceased in the United States. Nor was it long until foreign orders began to arrive for the refracting lenses of Alvan Clark & Sons. The fame of this firm went out through all the world, and by the beginning of the last quarter of the century the Clark instruments were regarded as the finest ever produced.

We cannot here refer to more than a few of the principal products of Clark & Sons. Gradually they extended the width of their lenses, gaining with each increase of diameter a rapidly increasing power of penetration. At last they produced for the Royal Observatory of Pulkova a twenty-seven-inch objective, which was, down to the early eighties, the master work of its kind in the world. It was in the grinding and polishing of their lenses that the Clarks surpassed all men. In the production of the glass castings for the lenses, the French have remained the masters. At the glass foundry of Mantois, of Paris, the finest and largest discs ever produced in the world are cast. But after the castings are made they are sent to America, to be made into those wonderful objectives which constitute the glory of the apparatus upon which the New Astronomy relies for its achievements.

It was in the year 1887 that the Lick Observatory on Mount Hamilton, of the Coast Range in Southern California, was completed. The lens of this instrument is thirty-six inches in diameter. Nor will the reader without reflection readily realize the enormous stride which was made in telescopy when the makers advanced from the twenty-seven-inch to the thirty-six-inch objective. Lenses are to each other in their power of collecting light and penetrating apace as the squares of their diameters, and in the extent of space explored as the cubes of their diameters.

The objective of the Pulkova instrument is to that of the Lick Observatory as 3 is to 4. The squares are as 9 is to 16, and the cubes are as 27 is to 64. This signifies that the depth of space penetrated by the Lick instrument is to that of its predecessor as 16 is to 9, and that the astronomical sphere resolved by the former is to the sphere resolved by the latter as 64 is to 27—that is, the Lick instrument at one bound revealed a universe *more than twice as great* as all that was known before! The human mind at this one bound found opportunity to explore and to know a sidereal sphere more than twice as extensive as had ever been previously penetrated by the gaze of man.

Nor is this all. The ambition of American astronomers and American philanthropists has not been content with even the prodigious achievement of the Lick telescope. In recent years an observatory has been projected in connection with the University of Chicago, which has come almost to completion, and which will bear by far the largest telescopic instrument in the world. The site selected for the observatory is seventy-five miles from the city, on the northern shore of Lake Geneva. There is a high ground here, rising sufficiently into a clear atmosphere, nearly two hundred feet above the level of the lake.

The observatory and the great telescope which constitutes its central fact are to bear the name of the donor, Mr. Yerkes, of Chicago, who has contributed the means for rearing this magnificent adjunct of the University. The enterprise contemplated from the first the construction of the most powerful telescope ever known. The manufacture of the objective, upon which everything depends, was assigned to Mr. Alvan G. Clark, of Cambridgeport, Massachusetts, who is the only living representative of the old firm of Alvan Clark & Sons.

Alvan G. Clark has inherited much of the genius of his father, though it is said that in making the lens of the Lick Observatory the father had to be called from his retirement to superintend personally some of the more delicate parts of the finishing before which task his sons had quailed. But the younger Clark readily agreed to make the Geneva lens, under the order of Yerkes, and to produce a perfect objective *forty inches in diameter*! This important work, so critical—almost impossible—has been successfully accomplished.

The making and the mounting of the Yerkes telescope have been assigned to Warner & Swasey, of Cleveland, Ohio, who are recognized as the best telescope builders in America. The great observatory is approaching completion. The instrument itself has been finished, examined, accepted by a committee of experts, and declared to fulfill all of the conditions of the agreement between the founder and the makers. Thus, just north of the boundary line between Illinois and Wisconsin, the greatest telescope of the world has been lifted to its dome and pointed to the heavens.

The formal opening of the observatory is promised for the summer months of 1896. The human mind by this agency has made another stride into the depths of infinite space. Another universe is presently to be penetrated and revealed. A hollow sphere of space outside of the sphere already known is to be added to the already unthinkable universe which we inhabit. Every part of the immense observatory and of the telescope is of American production, with the single important exception of the cast glass disc from which the two principal lenses, the one double convex and the other plano-concave, are produced. These were cast by Mantois, of Paris, whose superiority to the American manufacturers of optical glass is recognized.

It is estimated that the Yerkes telescope will gather three times as much light as the twenty-three-inch instrument of the Princeton Observatory. It surpasses in the same respect the twenty-six-inch telescope at the National Observatory in the ratio of two and three-eighths to one. It is in the same particular one and four-fifth times as powerful as the instrument of the Royal Russian Observatory at Pulkova; and it surpasses the great Lick instrument by twenty-three per cent.

What the practical results of the study of the skies through this monster instrument will be none may predict. Theoretically it is capable of bringing the moon to an apparent distance of sixty miles. Under favorable circumstances the observer will be able to note the characteristics of the lunar landscape with more distinctness than a good natural eye can discern the outlines and character of the summit of Pike's Peak from Denver. The instrument has sufficient power to reveal on the lunar disc any object five hundred feet square. Such a thing as a village or even a great single building would be plainly discernible.

Professor C.A. Young has recently pointed out the fact that the Yerkes telescope, if it meets expectation, will show on the moon's surface with much distinctness any such object as the Capitol at Washington. It is complained that in America wealth is selfish and self-centred; that the millionaire cares only for himself and the increase of his already exorbitant estate. The ambition of such men as Lick of San Jose and Yerkes of Chicago, seems to ameliorate the severe judgment of mankind respecting the holders of the wealth of the world, and even to transform them from their popular character of enemies and misers into philanthropists and benefactors.

# THE NEW ASTRONOMY

This century has been conspicuous above all centuries for new things. Man has grown into new relations with both nature and thought. He has interpreted nearly everything into new phraseology and new forms of belief. The scientific world has been revolutionized. Nothing remains in its old expression. Chemistry has been phrased anew. The laws of heat, light and electricity have been either revised or discovered wholly out of the unknown. The concept of universal nature has been so translated and reborn that a philosopher coming again out of the eighteenth century would fail to understand the thought and speech of even the common man.

In no other particular has the change been more marked than with respect to the general theory of the planetary and stellar worlds. A New Astronomy has come and taken the place of the old. The very rudiments of the science have to be learned as it were in a new language, and under the laws and theories of a new philosophy. Nature is considered from other points of view, and the general course of nature is conceived in a manner wholly different from the beliefs of the past.

In a preceding study we have explained the general notion of planetary formation according to the views of the last century. The New Astronomy presents another theory. Beginning with virtually the same notion of the original condition of our world and sun cluster, the new view departs widely as to the processes by which the planets were formed, and extends much further with respect to the first condition and ultimate destiny of our earth. The New Astronomy, like the old, begins with a nebular hypothesis. It imagines the matter now composing the solar group to have been originally dispersed through the space occupied by our system, and to have been in a state of attenuation under the influence of high heat. Out of this condition of diffusion the solar system has been evolved. The idea is a creation by the process of evolution; it is evolution applied to the planets. More particularly, the hypothesis is that the worlds of our planetary system grew into their present state through a series of stages and slow developments extending over æons of time.

This is the notion of world-growth substituted for that of world-production en masse by the action of centrifugal force and discharge from the solar equator. The New Astronomy proposes in this respect two points of remarkable difference from the view formerly entertained. The first relates to the fixing of the planetary orbits, and the other to the process by which the planets have reached their present mass and character. The old theory would place a given world in its pathway around the sun by a spiral flinging off from the central body, and would allow that the aggregate mass of the globe so produced was fixed once for all at the beginning. The new theory supposes that a given planetary orbit, as for instance that of the earth, was marked in the nebula of our system before the system existed—that is, that our orbit had its place in the beginning just as it has now; that the orbit was not determined by solar revolution and centrifugal action, but that it was mathematically existent in the nebular sheet out of which the solar system was produced.

Other lines existed in the same sheet of matter. One of these lines or pathways was destined for the orbit of Mercury; another for the orbit of Venus. One was for the pathway of Mars; another for the belt of the asteroids; another for Jupiter; another for Saturn, and still two others, far off on the rim, for Uranus and Neptune. The theory continues that such are the laws of matter that these orbital lines *must* exist in a disc of fire mist such as that out of which our solar universe has been produced. The New Astronomy holds firmly to the notion that the orbits of the planets are as much a part of the system as the planets themselves, and that both orbit and planet exist in virtue of the deep-down mathematical formulæ on which the whole material universe is constructed.

Secondly, the New Astronomy differs from the old by a whole horizon in the notion of world-production. About the middle of the century the theory began to be advanced that the worlds *grew* by accretion of matter; that they grew in the very paths which they now occupy; that they began to be with a small aggregation of matter rushing together in the line or orbit which the coming planet was to pursue. The planetary matter was already revolving in this orbit and in the surrounding spaces. It was already floating along in a nebulous superheated form capable of condensation by the loss of heat, but in particular capable of growth and development by the fall of surrounding matter upon the forming globe. We must remember that in the primordial state the elements of a planet, as for instance our earth, were mixed together and held in a state of tenuity ranging all the way from solid to highly vaporized forms, and that these elements subsequently and by slow adjustment got themselves into something approximating their present state.

The New Astronomy contemplates a period when each of the planets was a germinal nucleus of matter around which other matter was precipitated, thus producing a kind of world-growth or accretion. Thus, for instance, our earth may be considered at a time when its entire mass would not, according to our measurement, have weighed a hundred pounds! It consisted of a nucleus around which extended, through a great space, a mass of attenuated planetary matter. The nucleus once formed the matter adjacent would precipitate itself by gravitation upon the surface of the incipient world. The precipitation would proceed as heat was given off into space. It was virtually a process of condensation; but the result appeared like growth.

To the senses a planet would seem to be forming itself by accretion; and so, indeed, in one sense it was; for the mass constantly increased. As the nucleus sped on in the prescribed pathway, it drew to itself the surrounding matter, leaving behind it an open channel. The orbit was thus cleared of the matter, which was at first merely nebular, and afterward both nebular and fragmentary. The growth at the first was rapid. With each revolution a larger band of space was swept clear of its material. With each passage of the forming globe the matter from the adjacent spaces would rush down upon its surface, and as the mass of the planet increased the process would be stimulated; for gravitation is proportional to the mass. At length a great tubular space would be formed, having the orbit of the earth for its centre, and in this space the matter was all swept up. The tube enlarged with each revolution, until an open way was cut through the nebular disc, and then from the one side toward Venus and from the other side toward Mars the space widened and widened, until the globe took approximately by growth its present mass of matter. The nebulous material was drawn out of the inter-planetary space where it was floating, and the shower of star dust on the surface of the earth became thinner and less frequent. In some parts of the orbit bands or patches of this material existed, and the earth in passing through such hands drew down upon itself the flying fragments of such matter as it continues to do to the present day. What are meteoric displays but the residue of the primordial showers by which the world was formed?

All this work, according to the New Astronomy, took place while our globe was still in a superheated condition. The mass of it had not yet settled into permanent form. The water had not yet become water; it was steam. The metals had not yet become metals; they were rather the vapor of metals. At length they were the liquids of metals, and at last the solids. So, also, the rocks were transformed from the vaporous through the liquid into the solid form—all this while the globe was in process of condensation. It grew smaller in mathematical measurements at the same time that it grew heavier by the accretion of matter. At last the surface was formed, and in time that surface was sufficiently cooled to allow the vapors around it to condense into seas and oceans and rivers. There were ages of superficial softness—vast epochs of mud—in which the living beings that had now appeared wallowed and sprawled.

We cannot trace the world-growth through all its stages but can only indicate them as it were in a sketch. The more important thing to be noted is the relation of our planet in process of formation to the great fact called life. Here the New Astronomy comes in again to indicate, theoretically at least, the philosophy of planetary evolution. Each planet seems to pass through a vast almost inconceivable period in which its condition renders life on its surface or in its structure impossible. Heat is at once the favoring and the prohibitory condition of life. Without heat life cannot exist; with too great heat life cannot exist. With an intermediate and moderate degree of heat many forms of animate and inanimate existence may be promoted.

These facts tend to show that every world has in its career an intermediate period which may be called the epoch of life. Before the epoch of life begins there is in the given world no such form of existence. There is matter only. Then at a certain stage the epoch of life begins. The epoch of life continues for a vast indeterminate period. No doubt in some of the worlds an epoch of life has been provided ten times as great, possibly a thousand times as great, as in other planets. After the epoch of life begins only certain forms of existence are for a while possible. Then other and higher forms succeed them, and then still higher. Thus the process continues until the highest—that is, the conscious and moral form of existence becomes possible, and that highest, that conscious, that moral form of being is ourselves.

This is not all. The epoch of life seems to be terminable at the further extreme by a planetary condition in which life is no longer possible. The New Astronomy indicates the coming of a condition in all the worlds when life must disappear therefrom and be succeeded by a lifeless state of worldhood. This may be called the epoch of death—that is, of world-death. It seems to be almost established by investigation and right reason that worlds die. They reach a stage in which they are lifeless. They cool down until the waters and gases that are on the surface and above the surface recede more and more into the surface and then into the interior, until they wholly disappear. Cold takes the throne of nature. Universal aridity supervenes, and all forms of vegetable and animate existence go away to return no more. They dwindle and expire. The conditions that have come are virtually conditions of death.

Whether the universe contains within itself, under the Almighty supervision, certain arrangements and laws by which the dead world can be again cast into the crucible and regenerated by liberation through the action of heat into its primordial state once more and go the same tremendous round of planet life, we know not. The conception of such a process, even the dream or vague possibility of it, is sufficiently sublime and fills the mind with a great delight in contemplating the possible cycles through which the material universe is passing.

At any rate, we may contemplate the three great stages of world-life with which we are already acquainted—that is, the birth stage, the epoch of life and the epoch of death. There is a birth, as also a life and a death of planets. Richard A. Proctor, of great fame, on one of his last tours of instructive lecturing among our people, had for his subject the "Birth and Death of Worlds." The theme was not dissimilar to that which has been here presented in outline. The birth, the life and the death of worlds! Such is a summary of that almost infinite history through which our earth is passing—the history which the globe is *making* on its way from its nebulous to its final state.

Such, if we mistake not, is the story epitomized—the life history in brief—of all the worlds of space. They have each in its order and kind, an epoch of the beginning, then an epoch of growth and evolution, then an epoch of life—toward which all the preceding planet history seems to tend—and finally an epoch of death which must, in the course of infinite time, swallow from sight each planet in its turn, or at least reduce each from that condition in which it is an arena of animated existence into that state where it is a frozen and desert clod, still following its wonted path through space, still shining with a cold but cheerful face, *like our moon*, upon the silent abysses of the universe.

---

# WHAT THE WORLDS ARE MADE OF

The present century was already well advanced before there was any solid ground for the belief that the worlds of space are made of analogous or identical materials. It was only with the invention of the spectroscope and the analysis of light that the material identity of universal nature was proved by methods which could not be doubted. The proof came by the spectroscope.

This little instrument, though not famed as is its lordly kinsman the telescope, or even regarded with the popular favor of the microscope, has nevertheless carried us as far, and, we were about to say, taught us as much, as either of the others. It is one thing to see the worlds afar, to note them visibly, to describe their outlines, to measure their mass and determine their motions. It is another thing to know their constitution, the substances of which they are composed, the material condition in which they exist and the state of their progress in worldhood. The latter work is the task of the spectroscope; and right well has it accomplished its mission.

The solar spectrum has been known from the earliest ages. When the sun-bow was set on the background of cloud over the diluvial floods, the living beings of that age saw a spectrum—the glorious spectrum of rain and shine. Wherever the rays of light have been diffracted under given conditions by the agency of water drops, prism of glass or other such transparent medium, and the ray has fallen on a suitable screen, lo! there has been the beautiful spectrum of light.

The artificial, intentional production of this phenomenon of light has long been known, and both novice and scientist have tested and improved the methods of getting given results. The child's soap-bubble shows it in miniature splendor. The pressure of one wet pane of glass against another reveals it. The breakage of nearly all crystalline substances brings something of the colored effects of light; but the triangular prism of glass, suitably prepared, best of all displays the analysis of the sun-beam into the colors of which it is composed.

The spectroscope is the improved instrument by which the diffracting prism is best employed in producing the spectrum. The reader no doubt has seen a spectroscope, and has observed its beautiful work. In this place we pass, however, from the instrument of production to the spectrum, or analyzed result, as the same is shown on a screen. There the pencil of white light falling from the sun is spread out in the manner of a fan, presenting on the screen the following arrangement of colors: red, orange, yellow, green, blue, indigo and violet.

This order of colors, beginning with red, starts from that side of the spectrum which is least bent from the right line in which the white ray was traveling. The violet rays are most bent. The red rays are thus said to be at the *lower* edge of the prism, and the violet rays at the *upper* edge. Below the red rays there are now known to be certain invisible rays, as of heat and electricity. Above the violet rays are other invisible rays, such as the actinic influence. In fact, the spectrum, beginning invisibly, passes by way of the visible rays to the invisible again. Nor can any scientist in the world say at the present time *how much* is really included in the spread-out fan of analyzed sunlight.

Thus much scientists have known for some time. Certain other facts, however, in connection with the solar spectrum are of greater importance than are its more sensible phenomena. It was in the year 1802 that the English physicist, William Hyde Wollaston, discovered that the solar spectrum is crossed with a large number of *dark lines*. He it was who first mapped these lines and showed their relative position. He it was also who discovered the existence of invisible rays above the violet. Twelve years afterward Joseph von Fraunhofer, of Munich, a German optician of remarkable talents, took up the examination of the Wollaston lines, and by his success in the investigation succeeded in attracting the attention of the world.

This second stage in scientific discovery is generally that which receives the plaudits of mankind. It was so in the case of Fraunhofer. His name was given to the dark lines in the solar spectrum, and the nomenclature is retained to the present time. They are called the "Fraunhofer lines." It was soon discovered that the lines in question as produced in the spectrum are due to the presence of gases in the producing flame or source of light. It was also discovered that each substance in, the process of combustion yields its own line or set of lines. These appear at regular intervals in the spectrum. When several substances are consumed at the same time; the lines of each appear in the spectrum. The result is a *system* of lines, becoming more and more complex as the number of elements in the consuming materials is increased.

The lines in a narrow spectrum fall so closely together that they cannot be critically examined; but when more than one prism is used and the spectrum by this means spread out widely, the dark lines are made to stand apart. They are then found to number many thousands. We speak now of the analysis of sunlight. Experimentation was naturally turned, however, to terrestrial gases and solids on fire, and it was found that these also produce like series of dark lines in the spectrum. Or when the substances are consumed *as solids*, then the spectral effects are reversed, and the lines that would be dark lines in the luminous colored spectrum become themselves luminous lines on the screen; but these lines hold the same relation in mathematical measurement, etc., as do the *dark* lines in the colored spectrum.

Skillful spectroscopists succeeded in detecting and delineating the lines that were peculiar to each substance. By burning such substances in flame, they were able to produce the lines, and thus verify results. By such experimentation the various lines present in the solar spectrum were separated from the complex result, and the conclusion was reached that in the burning surface of the sun certain substances *well known on earth are present*; for the lines of those substances are shown in the spectrum.

No other known substances would produce the given lines. The conclusion is overwhelming that the substances in question are present in a gaseous condition in the burning flames of the sun. Down to the present time the examination of the sun's atmosphere has shown the existence therein of thirty-six known elements. These include sodium, potassium, calcium, magnesium, iron, copper, cobalt, silver, lead, tin, zinc, titanium, aluminium, chromium, silicon, carbon, hydrogen and several others.

It was thus established that in the constitution of the sun many of the well-known elements of the earth are present. There could be no mistake about it. An identity of lines in such a case proved beyond dispute the identity of the substance from which such lines are derived. The existence of common materials in the central sphere of our system and in *one* of his attendant orbs—our own—could not be doubted. The discovery of such a fact led by immediate inference to the expectation and belief that the *other* planets were of like constitution, or in a word, that the whole solar system was essentially composed of identical materials.

As the inquiry proceeded, it was found, however, that the agreement in the lines of different spectra was not perfect. Lines would be found in the spectrum derived from one source that were not present in a spectrum derived from another source. Materials were therefore suggested as present in one body that were not present in another. Still further inquiry confirmed the belief that while there is a general uniformity in the materials of our solar system, the identity is not complete in all. An element is found in one part that may not be found in another. Hydrogen shows its line in the spectrum derived from every heavenly body that has been investigated; but not so aluminium or cobalt. Sodium, that is, the salt-producing base, is discovered everywhere, but not nickel or arsenium. The result, in a word, shows a certain variability in the distribution of solar and planetary matter, but a general identity of most.

The question next presented itself as to the character of the luminous bodies *beyond* the solar system. Of what kind of matter are the comets? Of what kind are the fixed stars? Of what kind are the nebulæ? Could the spectroscope be used in determining also the character of the materials in those orbs that we see shining in the depths of space? The instrument was turned in answer to these questions to the sidereal heavens. No other branch of science has been prosecuted in the after half of this century with more zeal and success than has the spectroscopic analysis of the fixed stars. These are known by the telescope to have the character of suns. The most general fact of the visible heavens is the plentiful distribution of suns. They sparkle everywhere as the so-called fixed stars. To them the telescope has been virtually turned in vain. We say in vain because no single fixed star has, we believe, ever been made by aid of the telescope to show a disc.

On turning the telescope to a fixed star, its brightness, its brilliancy, increases according to the power of the instrument. Coming into the field of one of these great suns of space, the telescope shows a miraculous dawn spreading and blazing into a glorious sunrise, and a sun itself flaming like infinite majesty on the sight; but there is no disc—nothing but a blaze of glory. Thus in a sense the telescope has worked in vain on the visible heavens. But not so the spectroscope. The latter has done its glorious work. Turning to a given fixed star, it shows that the tremendous combustion going on therein is virtually the same as that in our own sun. There, too, is flaming hydrogen, and there is carbon and oxygen and iron and sodium and potassium and many other of the leading elements of what we thus know to be universal nature. The suns are all akin; they are cousins-german. They are of the same family—they and their progeny. They were born of the same universal fact. They are of the same Father! They are builded on the same plan, and they have a common destiny. Aye, more, the nebulæ that float far off, swanlike, in the infinitudes, are of the same family. The nebulæ may be regarded as the mothers of universes. It is out of their bosoms that the life and substance of all suns and worlds are drawn! And these, too, are composed of the common matter of universal nature. It is the same matter that we eat and drink. It is the same that we breathe. It is the same that we see aflame in our lamps and grates. It is the same that is borne to us in the fragrance of flowers planted on the graves of our dead. It is the common hydrogen and carbon and oxygen and nitrogen of our earth and its envelope. It is the soda of our bread; the potassa of our ashes; the phosphorus of our bones and brain! Indeed, the universe throughout is of one form and one substance, and there is one Father over all. Sooner or later the concepts of science and of religion will come together; and the small agitations and conflicts of human thought and hope will pass away in a sublime unity of human faith.

# Progress in Discovery and Invention

# THE FIRST STEAMBOAT AND ITS MAKER

On the night of the second of July, 1798, a man at a little old tavern in Bardstown, Kentucky, committed suicide. If ever there was a justifiable case of self-destruction, it was this. No human being is permitted to take his own life, but there are instances in which the burden of existence becomes well-nigh intolerable. In the case just mentioned, the man went to his room and took poison. He was a little more than fifty-five years of age, but was prematurely old from the hardships to which he had been subjected. He had not a penny. His clothes were worn out. A dirty shirt, made of coarse materials, was seen through the rags of his coat. His face was haggard, wrinkled, written all over with despair, the lines of which not even the goodness of death was able to dispel.

The man had seen the Old World and the New, but had never seen happiness. He had followed his forlorn destiny from his native town of South Windsor, Connecticut, where he was born on the twenty-first of January, 1743. His body was buried in the graveyard of Bardstown, then a frontier village. No one contributed a stone to mark the grave. Nor has that duty ever been performed. The spot became undistinguishable as time went by, and we believe that there is not a man in the world who can point out the place where the body of John Fitch was buried. The grave of the inventor of the steamboat, hidden away, more obscurely than that of Jean Valjean in the cemetery of Père-Lachaise, will keep the heroic bones to the last day, when all sepulchres of earth shall set free their occupants and the great sea's wash cast up its dead!

The life of John Fitch is, we are confident, the saddest chapter in human biography. The soul of the man seems from the first to have gone forth darkly voyaging, like Poe's raven,

—"Whom unmerciful disasterFollowed fast and followed faster, till his song one burden bore,Till the dirges of his hope the melancholy burden bore,—Of 'Nevermore—nevermore!'"

Certainly it was nevermore with him. His early years were made miserable by ill-treatment and abuse. His father, a close-fisted farmer and an elder brother of the same character, converted the boyhood life of John Fitch into a long day of grief and humiliation and a long night of gloomy dreams. Then at length came an ill-advised and ill-starred marriage, which broke under him and left him to wander forth in desolation.

He went first from Connecticut to Trenton, N.J., and there in his twenty-sixth year began to ply the humble trade of watch-maker. Then he became a gunsmith, making arms for the patriots of Seventy-six, until what time the British destroyed his shop. Then he was a soldier. He suffered the horrors of Valley Forge; and before the conclusion of the peace he went abroad in the country as a tinker of clocks and watches. His peculiarity of manner and his mendicant character made him the butt of neighborhoods. In 1780 he was sent as a deputy-surveyor from Virginia into Kentucky, and after nearly two years spent in the country between the Kentucky and Green rivers, he went back to Philadelphia. On a second journey to the West his party was assailed by the Indians at the mouth of the Muskingum, and most were killed. But he was taken captive, and remained with the red men for nearly a year. But he escaped at last, and got back to a Pennsylvania settlement.

Fitch next lived for a year or two in and did approve of the invention, he withheld any public endorsement of it.

Month after month went by, and no helping hand was extended. Fitch got the reputation of being a crazy man. To save himself from starvation, he made a map of the territory Northwest of the river Ohio, doing the work of the engraving with his own hand, and printing the impressions on a cider-press! Early in 1787 he succeeded in the formation of a small company; and this company supplied, or agreed to supply, the means requisite for the building of a steamboat sixty tons' burden. The inventor also secured patents from New Jersey, New York, Pennsylvania, Delaware and Virginia, granting to him the exclusive right to use the waters of those States for fourteen years for purposes of steam navigation.

Hereupon a boat was built and launched in the Delaware. It was forty-five feet in length and twelve feet beam. There were six oars, or paddles on each side. The engine had a twelve-inch cylinder, and the route of service contemplated was between Philadelphia and Burlington. The inventor agreed that his boat should make a rate of eight miles an hour, and the charge for passage should be a shilling.

He who might have been in Philadelphia on the twenty-second of August, 1787, and did approve of the invention, he withheld any public endorsement of it.

Month after month went by, and no helping hand was extended. Fitch got the reputation of being a crazy man. To save himself from starvation, he made a map of the territory Northwest of the river Ohio, doing the work of the engraving with his own hand, and printing the impressions on a cider-press! Early in 1787 he succeeded in the formation of a small company; and this company supplied, or agreed to supply, the means requisite for the building of a steamboat sixty tons' burden. The inventor also secured patents from New Jersey, New York, Pennsylvania, Delaware and Virginia, granting to him the exclusive right to use the waters of those States for fourteen years for purposes of steam navigation.

Hereupon a boat was built and launched in the Delaware. It was forty-five feet in length and twelve feet beam. There were six oars, or paddles on each side. The engine had a twelve-inch cylinder, and the route of service contemplated was between Philadelphia and Burlington. The inventor agreed that his boat should make a rate of eight miles an hour, and the charge for passage should be a shilling.

He who might have been in Philadelphia on the twenty-second of August, 1787, would have witnessed a memorable thing. The Convention for the framing of a Constitution for the United States of America was in session. For some time the body had been wearing itself into exhaustion over this question and that question which seemed impossible of solution. On the day referred to, the convention, on invitation, adjourned, and the members, including the Father of his country, who was President, went down to the water's edge to see a sight. There Fitch's steamboat was to make its trial trip, and there the trial trip was made, with entire success.

They who were building the ship of state could but applaud the performance of the little steamer that sped away toward Burlington. But the applause was of that kind which the wise and conservative folk always give to the astonishing thing done by genius. The wise and conservative folk look on and smile and praise, but do not commit themselves. Most dangerous it is for a politician to commit himself to a beneficial enterprise; for the people might oppose it!

The facts here referred to are fully attested in indisputable records. There are files of Philadelphia newspapers which contain accounts of Fitch's boat. A line of travel and traffic was established between Philadelphia and Burlington. There was also a steam ferryboat on the Delaware. A second boat, called the "Perseverance," was designed for the waters of the Mississippi; but this craft was wrecked by a storm, and then the patent under which the Ohio river and its confluent waters were granted, expired, and the enterprise had to be abandoned. On the fourth of September, 1790, the following advertisement of the "Pennsylvania Packet" appeared in a Philadelphia paper:

"The Steamboat will set out this morning, at eleven o'clock, for Messrs. Gray's Garden, at a quarter of a dollar for each passenger thither. It will afterwards ply between Gray's and middle ferry, at 11d each passenger. To-morrow morning, Sunday, it will set off for Burlington at eight o'clock, to return in the afternoon."

This Pennsylvania Packet continued to ply the Delaware for about three years. The mechanical construction of the boat was not perfect; and shortly after the date to which the above advertisement refers the little steamer was ruined by an accident. The story is told by Thomas P. Cope, in the seventh volume of Hazard's *Register.* He says: "I often witnessed the performance of the boat in 1788-89-90. It was propelled by paddles in the stern, and was constantly getting out of order. I saw it when it was returning from a trip to Burlington, from whence it was said to have arrived in little more than two hours. When coming to off Kensington, some part of the machinery broke, and I never saw it in motion afterward. I believe it was his [Fitch's] last effort. He had, up to that period, been patronized by a few stout-hearted individuals, who had subscribed a small capital, in shares, I think, of six pounds Pennsylvania currency; but this last disaster so staggered their faith and unstrung their nerves, that they never again had the hardihood to make other contributions. Indeed, they already rendered themselves the subjects of ridicule and derision for their temerity and presumption in giving countenance to this wild projector and visionary madman. The company thereupon gave up the ghost, the boat went to pieces, and Fitch became bankrupt and brokenhearted. Often have I seen him stalking about like a troubled spectre, with downcast eye and lowering countenance, his coarse, soiled linen peeping through the elbows of a tattered garment."

With the breakdown of his enterprise, John Fitch went forth penniless into the world. The patent which he received from the United States in 1791, was of small use. How little can a pauper avail himself of a privilege! Presently his patent was burned up, and a year afterward, namely in 1793, he went to France. There he would—according to his dream—find patronage and fame; but on his arrival in the French capital he found the Reign of Terror just beginning its work. It was not likely that the Revolutionary Tribunal would give heed to an American dreamer and his proposition to propel by steam a boat on the Seine. However, Fitch went to L'Orient and deposited the plans and specifications of his invention with the American consul. Then he departed for London.

In the following year a man by the name of Robert Fulton took up his residence with the family of Joel Barlow, in Paris. There he devoted himself to his art, which was that of a painter. Whoever had passed by the corner of Second and Walnut streets, in Philadelphia while Fitch was constructing his first steamboat, might have seen a little sign carrying these words: "Robert Fulton, Miniature Painter." But now, after nearly ten years, he was painting a panorama in France. While thus engaged, the American consul at L'Orient showed to Fulton Fitch's drawings and specifications for a steamboat. More than this, *he loaned them to him, and he kept them for several months.*

A thrifty man was Robert Fulton; discerning, prudent and capable! Meanwhile, poor Fitch, in 1794, returned to America. On the ship he worked his way as one of the hands. Getting again to New York he determined to make his way into that region of country where he had been a surveyor in 1780. He accordingly set out from New York for Kentucky, but not till he had invented, or rather constructed, a steamboat, which was driven by *a screw propeller*! This, in 1796, he launched on the Collect Pond, in what is now Lower New York. The boat was successful as an experiment; but the people who saw it looked upon its operation and upon the thing itself as the product of a crazy man's brain.

He who now passes along the streets of the metropolis will come upon a vendor of toys, who will drop upon the pavement an artificial miniature tortoise, rabbit, rat, or what not, well wound up; and the creature will begin to crawl, or dance, or jump, or run, according to its nature. The busy, conservative man smiles a superior smile, and passes on. It was in such mood that the old New Yorker of 1796 witnessed the going of Fitch's little screw propeller on the Pond. It was a toy of the water.

After this the poor spectre left for the West. The spring of 1798 found him at Bardstown, with the model of a little three-foot steamboat, which he launched on a neighboring stream. There he still told his neighbors that the time would come when all rivers and seas would be thus navigated. But they heeded not. The spectre became more spectral. At last, about the beginning of July, in the year just named, he gave up the battle, crept into his room at the little old tavern, took his poison, and fell into the final sleep.

We shall conclude this sketch of him and his work with one of his own sorrowful prophecies: "The day will come," said he in a letter, "when some more powerful man will get fame and riches from *my* invention; but nobody will believe that poor John Fitch can do anything worthy of attention." Than this there is, we think, hardly a more pathetic passage in the history of the sons of men!

# TELEGRAPHING BEFORE MORSE

There is a great fallacy in the judgment of mankind about the method of the coming of new things. People imagine that new things come all at once, but they do not. Nothing comes all at once; that is, no thing. In the facts of the natural world, that is, among visible phenomena of the landscape, the judgment of people is soon corrected. There it is seen that everything grows. The growth is sometimes slow and sometimes rapid; but everything comes gradually out of its antecedents. No tree or shrub or flower ever came immediately. No living creature on the face of the earth begins by instantaneous apparition. The chick gets out of its shell presently, but even that takes time. Every living thing comes on by degrees from a germ, and the germ is generally microscopic! Nature is, indeed, a marvel!

The facts of human life, whether tangible or intangible, have this same method. For example, there has not been an invention known to mankind that has not come on in the manner of growth. The antecedents of it work on and on in a tentative way, producing first this trial result and then that, always approaching the true thing; and even the true thing when it comes is not perfect. It is made perfect afterward. There was never an instantaneous invention, and there was never a complete one! It is doubtful whether there is at the present time a single complete, that is perfect or perfected, invention in the world. They are all of partial development. They show in their history their origin, their growth, their gradual approximation to the perfect form.

All of the marvelous contrivances which, fill the arena of our civilization, making it first vital and then vocal, have come by the evolutionary process. Every one of them has a history which is more and more obscure as we follow it backward to its source. In every case, however, there comes a time when a given discovery, manifesting itself in a given invention, takes a sort of spectacular character, and it is then rather suddenly revealed to the consciousness of mankind.

Of this general law the telegraph affords a conspicuous example. The whole world knows the story of the telegraph of Morse. It was in 1844 that the work of this great inventor was publicly demonstrated to the world. Then it was that the electro-magnetic telegraph in its first rude estate began to be used in the transmission of messages and other written information.

It has come to pass that "telegraph" means virtually *electric* telegraph. The people of to-day seem to have forgotten that the telegraph is not necessarily dependent on the electrical current. They have forgotten that back of the

Morse invention other means had been employed of transmitting information at a distance. They have forgotten that it was by the most gradual and tedious process that the old telegraphic methods were evolved into the new. Note with wonder how this great invention began, and through what stages it passed to completion.

There is a natural telegraphy. Whoever stands in an open place and calls aloud to his fellow mortal at a distance *telegraphs* to him. At least he telephones to him; that is, *sounds* to him at a distance. The air is the medium, the vocal cords in vibration the source of the utterance, and the ear of the one at a distance the audiphonic receiver. This sort of telegraphy is original and natural with human beings, and it is common to them and the lower animals. All the creatures that have vocality use this method. It were hard to say how humble is the creeping thing that does not rasp out some kind of a message to its fellow insect. Some, like the fireflies, do their telegraphing with a lantern which they carry. The very crickets are expert in telegraphy, or telephony, which is ultimately the same thing.

After transmitted sound the next thing is the visible signal, and this has been employed by human beings from the earliest ages in transmitting information to a distance. It is a method which will perhaps never be wholly abandoned. Observe the surveyors running a trial line. Far off is the chain bearer and here is the theodolite. The man with the standard watches for the signal of the man with the instrument. The language is *seen* and the message understood, though no word is spoken. Here the sunlight is the wire, and the visible motion of the hands and arms the letters and words of the message.

The ancients were great users of this method. They employed it in both peace and war. They occupied heights and showed signals at great distances. The better vision of those days made it possible to catch a signal, though far off, and to transmit it to some other station, likewise far away. In this manner bright objects were waved by day and torches by night. In times of invasion such a method of spreading information has been used down to the present age. Nor may we fail to note the improved apparatus for this kind of signaling now employed in military operations. The soldiers on our frontiers in Arizona, New Mexico, and through the mountainous regions further north, are able to signal with a true telegraphic language to stations nearly a hundred miles away.

Considerable progress was made in telegraphy in the after part of the eighteenth century. This progress related to the transmission of visible messages through the air. In the time of the French Revolution such contrivance occupied the attention of military commanders and of governing powers. A certain noted engineer named Chappe invented at this epoch a telegraph that might be properly called successful. Chappe was the son of the distinguished French astronomer, Jean Chappe d'Auteroche, who died at San Lucar, California, in 1769. This elder Chappe had previously made a journey into Siberia, and had seen from that station the transit of Venus in 1761. Hoping to observe the recurring transit, eight years afterward, he went to the coast of our then almost unknown California, but died there as stated above.

The younger Chappe, being anxious to serve the Revolution, invented his telegraph; but in doing so he subjected himself to the suspicions of the more ignorant, and on one notable occasion was brought into a strait place—both he and his invention. The story of this affair is given by Carlyle in the second volume of his "French Revolution." One knows not whether to smile or weep over the graphic account which the crabbed philosopher gives of Chappe and his work in the following extract:

"What, for example," says he, "is this that Engineer Chappe is doing in the Park of Vincennes? In the Park of Vincennes; and onward, they say, in the Park of Lepelletier Saint-Fargeau, the assassinated deputy; and still onward to the Heights of Ecouen and farther, he has scaffolding set up, has posts driven in; wooden arms with elbow-joints are jerking and fugling in the air, in the most rapid mysterious manner! Citoyens ran up, suspicious. Yes, O Citoyens, we are signaling; it is a device, this, worthy of the Republic; a thing for what we will call far-writing without the aid of postbags; in Greek it shall be named Telegraph. '*Telégraphê sacre*,' answers Citoyenism. For writing to Traitors, to Austria?—and tears it down, Chappe had to escape and get a new legislative Decree. Nevertheless he has accomplished it, the indefatigable Chappe; this his Far-writer, with its wooden arms and elbow-joints, can intelligibly signal; and lines of them are set up, to the North Frontiers and elsewhither. On an Autumn evening of the Year Two, Far-writer having just written that Condè Town has surrendered to us, we send from the Tuileries Convention-Hall this response in the shape of a Decree: 'The name of Condè is changed to *Nord-Libre* (North Free). The Army of the North ceases not to merit well of the country.' To the admiration of men! For lo! in some half-hour, while the Convention yet debates, there arrives this new answer: 'I inform thee (*Je t'annonce*), Citizen President, that the Decree of Convention, ordering change of the name Condè into North Free; and the other, declaring that the Army of the North ceases not to merit well of the country, are transmitted and acknowledged by Telegraph. I have instructed my Officer at Lille to forward them to North Free by express.' Signed, Chappe."

This successful telegraph of Engineer Chappe was not an electric telegraph, but a sunlight telegraph. Is it in reality any more wonderful to use the electrical wave in the transmission of intelligible symbols than to use a wave of light? Such seems to have been the opinion of mankind; and the coming of the electric telegraph was long postponed. The invention was made by slow approaches. In our country the notion has prevailed that Morse did all—that others did nothing; but this notion is very erroneous.

We are not to suppose that the Chappe method of telegraphing became extinct after its first successful work. Other references to what we *suppose* to be the same instrument are found in the literature of the age. The wonder is that more was not written and more accomplished by the agency of Chappe's invention. In the fall of the year 1800, General Bonaparte, who had been in Egypt and the East, returned to Europe and landed at Frejus on his way to Paris, with the dream of universal dominion in his head. In the first volume of the *Memoirs of Napoleon Bonaparte*, his secretary M. de Bourrienne, writing of the return to France says:

"We arrived in Paris on the 24th Vendemiaire (the sixteenth of October). As yet he (Napoleon) knew nothing of what was going on; for he had seen neither his wife nor his brothers, who were looking for him on the Burgundy Road. The news of our landing at Frejus had reached Paris *by a telegraphic despatch*. Madame Bonaparte, who was dining with M. Gohier when that despatch was communicated to him, as President of the Directory, immediately set off to meet her husband," etc. We should be glad to know in what particular form that "telegraphic despatch" was delivered! But such are Bourrienne's words!

To the American reader the name of Karl Friedrich Gauss may have an unfamiliar sound. Gauss was already a youth of fourteen when Morse was born, though the latter outlived the German mathematician by seventeen years. Gauss was a professor of Mathematics at Göttingen, where he passed nearly the whole of his life. In the early part of the century he distinguished himself in astronomy and in other branches of physical science. He then became interested in magnetic and electrical phenomena, and in 1833, with the assistance of Wilhelm Eduard Weber, one of his fellow-professors, who died in 1891, he erected at Göttingen a magnetic observatory. There he began to experiment with the subtle agent which was soon to be placed at the service of mankind.

The observatory was constructed without the use of iron, in order that the magnetic phenomena might be studied under favorable conditions. Humboldt and Arago had previously constructed laboratories without using iron—for iron is the great disturber—and from them Gauss obtained his hint. Weber was also expert in the management of magneto-electrical currents. Gauss, with the aid of his co-worker, constructed a line of telegraph, and sent signals by the agency of the magnetic current to a neighboring town. This was nearly ten years before Morse had fully succeeded in like experimentation.

It appears that the German scientists regarded their telegraph as simply the tangible expression or apparatus to illustrate scientific facts and principles. It was for this reason, we presume, that no further headway was made at Göttingen in the development of telegraphy. It was also for the additional reason that men rarely or never accept what is really the first demonstration and exemplification of a new departure in scientific knowledge. Such is the timidity of the human mind—such its conservative attachment to the known thing and to the old method as against the new—that it prefers to stay in the tumble-down ruin of bygone opinions and practices, rather than go up and inhabit the splendid but unfamiliar temple of the future.

Gauss and Weber were left with their scientific discovery; and, indeed, Morse in the New World of practicality and quick adaptations, was about to be rejected and cast out. The sorrows through which he passed need not here be recounted. They are sufficiently sad and sufficiently humiliating. His unavailing appeals to the American Congress are happily hidden in the rubbish of history, and are somewhat dimmed by the intervention of more than half a century. But his humiliation was extreme. Smart Congressmen, partisans, the ignorant flotsam of conventions and intrigues, heard the philosopher with contempt. A few heard him with sympathy; and the opinion in his favor grew, as if by the pressure of shame, until he was finally supported, and in a midnight hour of an expiring session of Congress, or rather in the early morning of the fourth of March, 1843, the munificent appropriation of $30,000 was placed at his disposal for the construction of an experimental line between Washington and Baltimore.

The one thing was done. A new era of instantaneous communication between men and communities at a distance the one from the other was opened—an era which has proved to be an era of light and knowledge. Nor may we conclude this sketch without noting the fact that, not a few of the members of the House of Representatives who voted the pittance for the construction of the first line of actual working telegraph in the world, went home to their constituents and were ignominiously beaten for re-election—this this for the slight service which they had rendered to their country and the human race!

When in New York City, turn thou to the west out of Fifth avenue into Twenty-second street, to the distance of, perhaps, ten rods, and there on a little marble slab set in the wall of a house on the north side of the street, read this curious epitaph:

"In this house lived Professor S.F.B, Morse for thirty years and died!"

# THE NEW LIGHT OF MEN

By the law of nature our existence is divided between daylight and darkness. There is evermore the alternate baptism into dawn and night. The division of life is not perfect between sunshine and shadow; for the sunshine bends around the world on both horizons, and lengthens the hemisphere of day by a considerable rim of twilight. To this reduction of the darkness we must add moonshine and starlight. But we must also subtract the influence of the clouds and other incidental conditions of obscuration. After these corrections are made, there is for mankind a great band of deep night, wherein no man can work. Whoever goes forth at some noon of night, when the sky is wrapped with clouds, must realize the utter dependence of our kind upon the light. How great is the blessing of that sublime and beautiful fact which the blind Milton apostrophizes in the beginning of the Third Book of *Paradise Lost*:

"Hail, holy Light! offspring of heaven first-born!Or of Eternal coëternal beam,May I express thee unblamed? since God is light,And never but in unapproached lightDwelt from eternity, dwelt then in thee,Bright effluence of bright essence increate!Or hear'st thou rather, pure ethereal stream,Whose fountain who shall tell? Before the sun,Before the heavens thou wert, and at the voiceOf God, as with a mantle, didst investThe rising world of waters dark and deep,Won from the void and formless infinite."

How then shall man overcome the darkness? It is one of the problems of his existence. He is obliged with each recurring sunset of his life to enter the tunnel of inky darkness and make his way through as best he may to the morning. What kind of lantern shall he carry as he gropes?

The evolution of artificial light and of the means of producing it constitutes one of the most interesting chapters in the history of our race. Primeval man knew fire. He learned in some way how to kindle fire. The lowest barbarian may be defined as a fire-producing animal. The cave men of ancient Europe kindled fires in their dark caverns. The lake dwellers had fires, both on shore and in their huts over the water. Wherever there was a fire there was artificial light. The primitive barbarian walked around the embers of his fire and saw his shadow stretching out into the gloom of the surrounding night.

With the slow oncoming of a better estate, the early philosophers of mankind invented lamps. Very rude indeed were the first products in this kind of art. Note the character of the lamps that have survived to us from the age of stone. Still they are capable of holding oil and retaining a wick. Further on we have lamps from the age of bronze, and at last from the age of iron. Polite antiquity had its silver lamps, its copper lamps, and in a few instances its lamps of gold. The palaces of kings were sometimes lighted from golden reservoirs of oil. Such may be seen among the relics preserved to us from the civilizations of Western Asia. The palace of Priam, if we mistake not, had lamps of gold.

The Great Greeks were the makers of beautiful lamps. In the age of the Grecian ascendancy the streets of Athens and of some other Hellenic cities were lighted by night. The material of such illumination was oil derived either from animals or from vegetable products, such as the olive. In the forms of Greek lamps we have an example of artistic beauty not surpassed or equaled in modern time; but the mechanical contrivance for producing the light was poor and clumsy.

Rome lighted herself artificially. She had her lamps and her torches and her chandeliers, as we see in the relics of Herculaneum and Pompeii. A Roman procession by night was not wanting in brilliancy and picturesqueness. The quality of the light, however was poor, and there was always a cloud of smoke as well as of dust hovering about Roman processions and triumphs.

The earlier Middle Ages improved not at all; but with the Renaissance there was an added elegance in the apparatus of illumination. Chandeliers were made in Italy, notably in Venice, that might rival in their elegance anything of the present age. The art of such products was superior; but the old barbaric clumsiness was perpetuated in the mechanical part. With the rise of scientific investigation under the influence of inductive philosophy, all kinds of contrivances for the production of artificial light were improved. The ingenuity of man was now turned to the mechanical part, and one invention followed another with a constant development in the power of illumination.

We can but remember, however, that until the present age many of the old forms of illuminating apparatus have been retained. In the ruder communities such things may still be seen. Civilization in its progress from east to west across our continent followed a tallow candle. The light of it was seen by night through the window of the pioneer's cabin. The old forms of hanging lamps have hardly yet disappeared from the advance posts of the marching column. But meanwhile, other agencies have been discovered, and other forms of apparatus invented, until the branch of knowledge relating to illumination has become both a science and an art.

Within the memories of men still living, a great transformation has occurred. Animal oils have virtually ceased to be employed as the sources of light. The vegetable world is hardly any longer drawn upon for its products. Already before the discovery of petroleum and its multifarious uses the invention by chemical methods of illuminating materials had begun. Many kinds of burning fluid had been introduced. The reign of these was short-lived; coal oil came in at the door and they flew out at the window. Great was the advantage which seemed to come to mankind from the use of kerosene lamps. Those very forms of illumination which are now regarded as crude in character and odious in use were only a generation ago hailed with delight because of their superiority to the former agents of illumination. Thus much may suffice for all that precedes the coming of the New Light of men. The new light flashes from the electrical glow. The application of electricity to purposes of illumination marks an era in human progress. The electrical light is, we think, high up among the most valuable and striking stages of civilized life in the nineteenth century. It is best calculated to affect favorably the welfare of the people, especially in great cities. The illumination of a city by night, making its streets to be lighted as if by day, is a more interesting and important fact in human history than any political conflict or mere change of rulers.

About the beginning of the eighth decade of this century the project of introducing the electric light for general purposes of illumination began to be agitated. It was at once perceived that the advantages of such lighting were as many as they were obvious. The light is so powerful as to render practicable the performance of many mechanical operations as easily by night as by day. Again, the danger of fire from illuminating sources is almost wholly obviated by the new system. The ease and expedition of all kinds of night employment are greatly enhanced. A given amount of illumination can be produced much more cheaply by electricity than by any means of gas lighting or ordinary combustion. Among the first to demonstrate the feasibility of electric lighting was the philosopher Gramme, of Paris. In the early part of 1875 he successfully lighted his laboratory by means of electricity. Soon afterward the foundry of Ducommun & Co., of Mulhouse, was similarly lighted. In the course of the following year the apparatus for lighting, by means of carbon candles was introduced into many of the principal factories of France and other leading countries of Europe. It may prove of interest in this connection to sketch briefly the principal features of the electric light system, and to trace the development of that system in our own and other countries.

Lighting by electricity is accomplished in several ways. In general, however, the principle by which the result is accomplished is one, and depends upon the resistance which the electrical current meets in its transmission through various substances. There are no perfect conductors of electricity. In proportion as the non-conductive quality is prevalent in a substance, especially in a metal, the resistance to the passage of electricity is pronounced, and the consequent disturbance among the molecular particles of the substance is great. Whenever such resistance is encounted in a circuit, the electricity is converted into heat, and when the resistance is great, the heat is, in turn, converted into light, or rather the heat becomes phenomenal in light; that is, the substance which offers the resistance glows with the transformed energy of the impeded current. Upon this simple principle all the apparatus for the production of electric light is produced.

Among the metallic substances, the one best adapted by its low conductivity to such resistance and transformation of force, is platinum. The high degree of heat necessary to fuse this metal adds to its usefulness and availability for the purpose indicated. When an electrical current is forced along a platinum wire too small to transmit the entire volume, it becomes at once heated—first to a red, and then to a white glow—and is thus made to send forth a radiance like that of the sun. Of the non-metallic elements which offer similar resistance, the best is carbon. The infusibility of this substance renders it greatly superior to platinum for purposes of the electric light.

Near the beginning of the present century it was discovered by Sir Humphry Davy that carbon points may be rendered incandescent by means of a powerful electrical current. The discovery was fully developed in the year 1809, while the philosopher just referred to was experimenting with the great battery of the Royal Institution of London. He observed—rather by accident than by design or previous anticipation—that a strong volume of electricity passing between two bits of wood charcoal produces tremendous heat, and a light like that of the sun. It appears, however, that Davy at first regarded the phenomenon rather in the nature of an interesting display of force than as a suggestion of the possibility of turning night into day.

For nearly three-quarters of a century the discovery made by Sir Humphrey lay dormant among the great mass of scientific facts revealed in the laboratory. In the course of time, however, the nature of the new fact began to be apprehended. The electric lamp in many forms was proposed and tried. The scientists, Niardet, Wilde, Brush, Fuller, and many others of less note, busied themselves with the work of invention. Especially did Gramme and Siemens devote their scientific genius to the work of turning to good account the knowledge now fully possessed of the transformability of the electric current into light.

The experiments of the last named two distinguished inventors brought us to the dawn of the new era in artificial lighting. The Russian philosopher, Jablokhkoff, carried the work still further by the practical introduction of the carbon candle. Other scientists—Carre, Foucault, Serrin, Rapieff, and Werdermann—had, at an earlier or later day, thrown much additional information into the common stock of knowledge relative to the illuminating possibilities of electricity. Finally, the accumulated materials of science fell into the hands of that untutored but remarkably radical inventor, Thomas A. Edison, who gave himself with the utmost zeal to the work of removing the remaining difficulties in the problem.

Edison began his investigations in this line of invention in September of 1878, and in December of the following year gave to the public his first formal statement of results. After many experiments with platinum, he abandoned that material in favor of the carbon-arc *in vacuo*. The latter is, indeed, the essential feature of the Edison light. A small semicircle, or horseshoe, of some substance, such as a filament of bamboo reduced to the form of pure carbon, the two ends being attached to the poles of the generating-machine, or dynamo, as the engine is popularly called, is enclosed in a glass bulb, from which the air has been carefully drawn, and is rendered incandescent by the passage of an electric current. The other important features of Edison's discovery relate to the divisibility of the current, and its control and regulation in volume by the operator. These matters were fully mastered in the Edison invention, and the apparatus rendered as completely subject to management as are the other varieties of illuminating agencies.

It were vain to speculate upon the future of electric lighting. The question of artificial illumination has had much to do with the progress of the human race, particularly when aggregated into cities. Doubtless the old systems of lighting are destined in time to give place altogether to the splendors of the electric glow. The general effect of the change upon society must be as marked as it is salutary. Darkness, the enemy of good government and morality in great cities, will, in great measure, be dispelled by the beneficent agent, over which the genius of Davy, Gramme, Brush, Edison, and a host of other explorers in the new continents of science has so completely triumphed. The ease, happiness, comfort, and welfare of mankind must be vastly multiplied, and the future must be reminded, in the glow that dispels the night, of that splendid fact that the progress of civilization depends, in a large measure, upon a knowledge of Nature's laws, and the diffusion of that knowledge among the people.

---

# THE TELEPHONE

Perhaps no other great invention of man has been within so short a period so widely distributed as the telephone. The use of the instrument is already co-extensive with civilization. The cost at which the instruments are furnished is still so considerable that the poor of the world are not able to avail themselves of the invention; but in the so-called upper circles of society the use of the telephone is virtually universal. It has made its way from the city to the town, from the town to the village, from the village to the hamlet, and even to the country-side where the millions dwell.

The telephone came by a speedy revelation. It was born of that intense scientific activity which is the peculiarity of our age. The antecedent knowledge out of which it sprang had existed in various forms for a long time. The laws of acoustics were among the first to be investigated after a true physical science began to be taught. The phenomena of sound are so universal and experimentation in sound production so easy, that the governing laws were readily discovered.

Acoustics, we think, foreran somewhat the science of heat, as the science of heat preceded that of light. Electricity came last. The telephone is an instrument belonging not wholly, not chiefly, but only in part, to acoustics. It owes its existence to magnetic induction and electrical transmission as much as to the mere action of sound. One foot of the instrument, so to speak, is acoustics, and the other foot electricity. The telephone philosophically considered is an instrument for the conversion of a sound-wave into electrical motion, and its reconversion into sound at a distance. The sound is, as it were, committed to the electrical current and is thus sent to the end of the journey, and there discharged with its message. The possibility of this result lies first of all in the fact of electrical transmission by wire, and in the second place to the mounting of a sound-rider on the electrical saddle for an instantaneous journey with important despatches!

New results in scientific progress generally seem marvelous. The unfamiliar and unexpected thing is always a marvel; but scientifically considered, the telephone does not seem so surprising as at first view. The atmosphere is a conductor of sound. It is the natural agent of transmission, and so far as the natural man is concerned, it is his only agent for the transmission of oral utterance. If the unlearned man have his attention called to the surprising fact of hearing his fellow-man call out to him across a field or from far off on the prairie, he does not think it marvelous, but only natural. Yet how strange it is that one human being can speak to another through the intervening space!

It is strange that one should see another at a distance; but seeing and hearing at distances are natural functions of living creatures. The sunlight is for one sense and the sound-wave is for the other. The sound-wave travels on the atmosphere, and preserves its integrity. A given sound is produced, and the same sound is heard by some ear at a distance. All the people of the world are telephoning to one another; for oral speech leaping from the vocal organs of one human being to the ear of another is always telephonic. It is only when this phenomenon of speech at a distance is taken from the soft wings of the air, confined to a wire, and made to fly along the slender thread and deliver itself afar in a manner to which the world has hitherto been a stranger that the thing done and the apparatus by which it is done seem miraculous. Indeed it is a miracle; for *miraculum* signifies wonderful.

The history of the invention of the telephone is easily apprehended. The scientific principles on which it depends may be understood without difficulty. There is, however, about the instrument and its action something that is well nigh unbelievable. It is essentially a thing contrary to universal experience, if not positively inconceivable, that the slight phenomenon of the human voice should be, so to speak, *picked up* by a physical contrivance, carried a thousand miles through a thread of wire not a quarter of an inch in diameter, and delivered in its integrity to the sense of another waiting to receive it! At all events, the history of the telephone, belonging so distinctly to our own age, will stand as a reminder to after times of the great stride which the human race made in inventive skill and scientific progress in the last quarter of the nineteenth century.

The telephone, like many similar instruments, was the work of several ingenious minds directed at nearly the same time to the same problem. The solution, however, must be accredited first of all to Elisha P. Gray, of Chicago, and Alexander Graham Bell, of the Massachusetts Institute of Technology. It should be mentioned, however, that Amos E. Dolbear, of Tufts College, Massachusetts, and Thomas A. Edison, of Menlo Park, New Jersey, likewise succeeded in solving the difficulty in the way of telephonic communication, and in answering practically several of the minor questions that hindered at first the complete success of the invention. The telephone is an instrument for the reproduction of sounds, particularly the sounds of the human voice, by the agency of electrical conduction at long distances from the origin of the vocal disturbance. Or it may be defined as an instrument for the *transmission* of the sounds referred to by the agencies described. Indeed it were hard to say whether in a telephonic message we receive a *reproduced* sound or a *transmitted* sound. On the whole, it is more proper to speak of a reproduction of the original sound by transmission of the waves in which that sound is first written.

It is now well known that the phenomenon called sound consists of a wave agitation communicated through the particles of some medium to the organ of hearing. Every particular sound has its own physical equivalent in the system of waves in which it is written. The only thing, therefore, that is necessary in order to carry a sound in its integrity to any distance, is to transmit its physical equivalent, and to redeliver that equivalent to some organ of hearing capable of receiving it.

Upon these principles the telephone was produced—created. Every sound which falls by impact upon the sheet-iron disk of the instrument communicates thereto a sort of tremor. This tremor causes the disk to approach and recede from the magnetic pole placed just behind the diaphragm. A current of electricity is thus induced, pulsates along the wire to the other end, and is delivered to the metallic disk of the second instrument, many miles away, just as it was produced in the first. The ear of the hearer receives from the second instrument the exact physical equivalent of the sound, or sounds, which were delivered against the disk of the first instrument, and thus the utterance is received at a distance just as it was given forth.

As already said, the invention of the telephone stands chiefly to the credit of Professors Gray and Bell. It should be recorded that as early as 1837, the philosopher Page succeeded, by means of electro-magnetism, in transmitting *musical* tones to a distance. It was not, however, until 1877 that Professer Bell, in a public lecture given at Salem, Mass., astonished his audience, and the whole country as well, by receiving and transmitting *vocal* messages from Boston, twenty miles away. Incredulity had no more a place as it respected the feasibility of talking to persons at a distance. The experiments of Gray at Chicago, a few days later in the same month, were equally successful. Messages were distinctly delivered between that city and Milwaukee, a distance of eighty-five miles, nor could it be longer doubted that a new era in the means of communication had come.

The Bell telephone, with its many modifications and improvements, has come into rapid use. Within reasonable limits of distance, the new method of transmitting intelligence by direct vocal utterance, has taken the place of all slower and less convenient means of intercommunication. The appearance of the simple instrument has been one of the many harbingers of the oncoming better time, when the interchange of thought and sentiment between man and man, community and community, nation and nation, and race and race shall be the preliminary of universal peace in the world and of the good-fellowship of mankind.

Every such fact as the invention of the telephone, produces a complex and almost indescribable result in human society. This result has in it, in the first place, a change in the manners and method of the individual There is also a change in his sentiments. He whose work in life, whatever it may be, is accomplished in touch with the telephone will realize that he is in touch with the whole world. This intimacy reaches, first, his neighbors and friends. He seems to live henceforth in their presence, and in communication with them.

The isolation of the individual life is virtually obliterated by such an agency. Solitude disappears before it; for he whose ear is within hearing of his instrument, knows not at what moment any one of many thousands of people may speak to him. He knows not at what moment intelligence of an ever-varying kind may be spoken to him from his own community or out of the depths of distance. The mind is thus affiliated with an enlarged and ever-present society. These considerations do not relate to mere matters of convenience and quickness and advantage and safety, but to the larger question of the aggregate effect upon the individual.

The effect on the community is of like kind. The community is no longer so segregated as it was before. The community is in touch with other communities of like character. The conflagration in one town is felt in the neighboring towns, if it is not seen. The epidemic of the one is the epidemic of many. The sensation of the one community diffuses itself instantly into several. The effect is in the intellectual life like that of a wave produced on the lake by the casting in of a stone. The wave widens and recedes. It may be obstructed or unobstructed in its progress. If obstructed, the obstructions may be removed. Then the motion of the wave will become free and regular. So also on the tide of public thought. The telephone is an agency *for removing mental obstructions*, and for the regular diffusion of a common thought.

All this, however, is attended with draw-backs. One of these is the breaking in on the privacy and seclusion of the individual life. Individuality suffers under scientific progress. Great thinking is accomplished best in solitude. Emerson has forcibly pointed out the advantages which arise in the intellectual life from its isolation and seclusion—from its free and uninterrupted communion with itself.

The convenience—the physical convenience—of life is vastly augmented by such a contrivance as the telephone. Time is saved and trouble obviated. But at the same time the necessity for bodily exercise is reduced, and the overgrowth of brain at the expense of body encouraged. The fact is that the invention of the telephone and its general use, while it has added very greatly to the comfort of life, while it has promoted ease and diffused a social sense that needed stimulation and development, has at the same time brought in conditions that are not wholly favorable to human welfare. More largely still, the truth is that the telephone, like every other symbol and agency of progress, has brought *enlarged responsibilities.*

No man, no community, no people or nation can gain an increase of power without accepting the accompanying increase of responsibility. The moral nature of man is thus involved. Every forward stride of scientific invention places upon the life of man, including his bodily activity, his mental moods and his spiritual and moral powers, an added stress of duty, of energy, and of rectitude in conduct from which he may not shrink if he would be the gainer rather than the loser. Each discovery and each improved method of employing the beneficent forces of the natural world, brings with it a strain upon the moral nature of man which, if he stand it, well; but if he stand it not, then it shall go ill with him.

# THE MACHINE THAT "TALKS BACK"

The invention for making nature give an intelligent response may well be regarded with wondering interest. The odd, we might say humorous, feature of the invention is that nature, being as it were cornered and compelled to respond, will answer nothing except *to repeat what is said in her ear!* The phonograph may be defined as a mechanical parrot. Unlike the living bird, however, it never makes answers malapropos. It never deviates from the original text. The distrust which has been justly cherished against the talking bird on account of his originality can never be reasonably directed against the phonograph!

The possibility of writing sound has been recognized for a century past. Since the discovery of the vibratory character of sound, the physicist has seen the feasibility of recording the vibration. Nature herself has given many hints along this line of experimentation. Long ago it was seen that the writing sand sprinkled on the sounding board of the piano would under the influence of a chord struck from the keys arrange itself in geometrical figures. It was also seen that a discord sounded from the key-board would break the figures into chaos and confusion. Were not these phenomena sufficient to suggest that sound might be written in intelligible characters?

The mind, however, moves slowly from the old to the new. The former concept of physical facts and the laws which govern them is not readily given up. A great discovery in physical science seems to disturb the foundations of nature. It does not really do so; the disturbance is not in nature, but in the mind. No endeavor of man, no advance of his from some old bivouac to a new camping-ground, affects in the least the order of the world. The change, we repeat, is in the man, and in the race to which he belongs.

Long and tedious has been the process of getting thought into a recorded form. The first method of expressing thought was oral. Long before any other method of holding ideas and delivering them to others was devised or imagined, speech came. Speech is oral. It is made of sound. Oral utterance is no doubt as old as the race itself. It began with the first coming of our kind into this sphere. Indeed we now know that the rudiments of speech exist in the faculties of the lower animals. The studies of Professor Garner have shown conclusively that the humble simian folk of the African forest have a speech or language. Of this the professor himself has become a student, and he claims to have learned at least sixty words of the vocabulary!

Strange it is to note the course which linguistic development has taken. At the first, there was a *spoken* language only. The next stage was to get this spoken language recorded, not in *audible*, but in *visible* symbols. Why should it have been so easy and apparently natural for the old races to invent a visible form of speech-writing rather than an audible form? Why should the ancients have fallen back on the eye rather than the ear as the sense to be instructed? Why should sight-writing have been invented thousands of years ago, and sound-writing postponed until the present day?

In any event, such has been the history of recorded language. The early races began as the mother begins with her children; that is, with oral speech. But at a certain stage this method was abandoned, and teachers came with pictorial symbols of words. They invented visible characters to signify words, syllables, sounds. Thus came alphabetical writing, syllabic writing, verbal writing, into the world. Ever afterward the children of men learned speech first from their parents, by oral utterance; but afterward by means of the pictorial signs in which human language was recorded.

This method became habitual. The eye was made to be the servant of the intellect in learning nearly all that was to be gained from the wisdom of the past. It was by the tedious way of crooked marks signifying words that ideas were henceforth gleaned out of human lore by all who would learn aught from the recorded wisdom of mankind. And yet there never was anything essentially absurd or insurmountable in the invention of a method of recording speech in audible instead of visible symbols.

The phonograph came swiftly after the telephone. The new instrument is in a sense the complement of its predecessor. Both inventions are based upon the same principle in science. The discovery that every sound has its physical equivalent in a wave or agitation which affects the particles of matter composing the material through which the sound is transmitted led almost inevitably to the other discovery of *catching* and *retaining* that physical equivalent or wave in the surface of some body, and to the reproduction of the original sound therefrom.

Such is the fundamental principle of the interesting but, thus far, little useful instrument known as the phonograph. The same was invented by Thomas A. Edison, of Menlo Park, in the year 1877. The instrument differs considerably in structure and purpose from the *Vibrograph* and *Phonautograph* which preceded it. The latter two instruments were made simply to *write* sound vibrations; the former, to reproduce *audibly* the sounds themselves.

The phonograph consists of three principal parts,—the sender or funnel-shaped tube, with its open mouth-piece standing toward the operator; the diaphragm and stylus connected therewith, which receives the sound spoken into the tube; and thirdly, the revolving cylinder, with its sheet-coating of tin-foil laid over the surface of a spiral groove to receive the indentations of the point of the stylus. The mode of operation is very simple. The cylinder is revolved; and the point of the stylus, when there is no sound agitation in the funnel or mouth-piece, makes a smooth, continuous depression in the tin-foil over the spiral groove. But when any sound is thrown into the mouth-piece the iron disk or diaphragm is agitated; this agitation is carried through the stylus and written in irregular marks, dots, and peculiar figures in the tin-foil over the groove.

When the utterance which is to be reproduced has been completed, the instrument is stopped, the stylus thrown back from the groove, and the cylinder revolved backward to the place of starting. The stylus is then returned to its place in the groove, and the cylinder is revolved forward at the same rate of rapidity as before. As the point of the stylus plays up and down in the indentations and through the figures in the tin-foil, produced by its own previous agitation, a quiver exactly equivalent to that which was produced by the utterance in the mouth-piece is thrown into the air. This agitation is of course the exact physical equivalent of the original sound, or, more properly, *is* the sound itself. Thus it is that the phonograph is made to talk, to sing, to cry; to utter, in short, any sound sufficiently powerful to produce a perceptible tremor in the mouth-piece and diaphragm of the instrument.

Much progress has been made toward the utilization of the phonograph as a practical addition to the civilizing apparatus of our time. It may be said, indeed, that all the difficulties in the way of such a result have been removed. Mr. Edison has carried forward his work to such a degree of perfection that the instrument may be practically employed in correspondence and literary composition. The problem has been to *stereotype*, so to speak, the tin-foil record of what has been uttered in the mouth-piece, and thus to preserve in a permanent form the potency of vanished sounds. Nor does it require a great stretch of the imagination to see in the invention of the phonograph one of the greatest achievements of the age—a discovery, indeed, which may possibly revolutionize the whole method of learning.

It would seem clear that nature has intended the *ear*, rather than the eye, to be the organ of education. It is manifestly against the fitness of things that the eyes of all mankind should be strained, weakened, permanently injured in childhood, with the unnatural tasks which are imposed upon the delicate organ. It would seem to be more in accordance with the nature and capacities of man, and the general character of the external world, to reserve the eye for the discernment and appreciation of beauty, and to impose upon the ear the tedious and hard tasks of education.

The phonograph makes it possible to read by the ear instead of by the eye, and it is not beyond the range of probability that the book of the future, near or remote, will be written in phonographic plates and made to reveal its story directly to the waiting ear, rather than through the secondary medium of print to the enfeebled and tired eye of the reader.

We hardly venture on prophecy; but we think that he who returns to this scene of human activity at the close of the twentieth century will find that sound has been substituted for sight in nearly everything that relates to recorded information, to learning, and to educational work. By that means the organ of hearing will be restored to its rightful office. Enlightenment and instruction of all kinds will be given by means of phonographic books. The sound-wave will, in a word, be substituted for the light-wave as the vehicle of all our best information and intercourse. The ear will have habitually taken the place of the eye in the principal offices of interest and information.

The unnatural method of the book—the visible book instead of the audible book—will then be done away. Nature, who instructs the child by sound, will continue to teach the man in the same manner. All mothers, from the mother bird to the mother woman, begin the teaching of their offspring by sound, by utterance. The mother bird continues in this manner; but the mother woman is presently supplanted by a teacher who comes in with a printed book filled with crooked marks, and would have it that learning must be *thus* acquired. Instead of continuing the natural process of instruction to the complete development and information of the mind, an abnormal method has been adopted by mankind with many hurtful consequences.

The youth at a certain age is led into the world of science, and there dismissed from the mother-method, to acquire, if he can, the painful and tedious use of meaningless hieroglyphics. There he must study with the eye, learning as best he may the significance of the crooked signs which can at the most signify no more than words. How much of human energy and life and thought have been thus wasted in the instruction of the mind by characters and symbols. The eyes of mankind have, as we said, been dimmed and shadowed, and at the same time the faculties have been overheated and the equipose of perception and memory seriously disturbed by this unnatural process of learning.

Human beings begin the acquirement of knowledge with words, and they end with words; but an unnatural civilization has taught man to walk the greater part of his intellectual journey by means of arbitrary systems of writing and printing. When the next Columbian Year arrives we shall see him untaught (a hard thing withal) and retaught on nature's plan of learning. Nature teaches language by sound only. Artificiality writes a scrawl. Nature's book is a book of words. Man's book is as yet a book of signs and symbols. Nature's book utters itself to the ear, and man's book blinds the eyes and overheats the imagination. Nature's method is to teach by the ear, and to reserve the sight for the discovery and enjoyment of beauty.

The sound-book in some form is coming; and with that the intellectual repose of mankind will begin to be restored. The use of the eye for the offices of education instead of the stronger ear, has, we think, impaired, if it has not destroyed, the equilibrium of the human mind. That equilibrium must be restored. The mental diseases and unrest of our race are largely attributable to the over-excitement of the faculties through ages of too much seeing.

The Age of Hearing is, we think, to be ushered in with the twentieth century. The coming of that age will tend to restore the mental balance of mankind. Memory, now almost obliterated, will come again. The over-heated perceptions will cool. The imagination will become calm, and the eye itself will recover, we hope, from the injuries, of overstrain, and will regain its power and lustre. Man will see once more as the eagle sees, and will learn Shakespeare by heart. He will remember all knowledge, and will again be able to see, as of old, from Sicily to Carthage!

# THE EVOLUTION OF THE DYNAMO

BY PROFESSOR JOSEPH P. NAYLOR, A.M.

It is difficult to estimate the influence in modifying and shaping the nineteenth century civilization that has resulted from the discovery of the dynamo and the production of heavy currents of electricity. That it has had great influence is evident without question. The arc light for out-of-doors lighting and the incandescent lamp for inside has modified all our previous ideas of illumination. Effects in light are now produced daily that were beyond imagination twenty years since. The trolley and the electromoter have largely solved the problem of rapid transit through our crowded cities. Thus larger business facilities, suburban homes and cheaper living, cleanliness and better sanitary conditions are electrical results.

The transmission of energy by the electric current from a central plant makes possible many small industries that could not exist without it, and gives employment and happiness to hundreds. The art of Electro-metallurgy seems but the development of months: yet it already employs millions of capital and is adding thousands daily to the world's wealth. Steam and wind and tide contribute to the work. Even Niagara is being touched by the spirit of the time and sends her wasting energy thrilling through the electric wires to turn the wheels of many busy factories. It is perhaps not the least remarkable fact in connection with this work that it is largely the product of the last thirty years, and that it had its very beginning less than seventy years since. Edison and Thompson and Brush are honorable household names; yet they are still living to produce even greater electric marvels. In fact, so rapid and brilliant has been the development that in the brilliancy some of the pioneers in the work have been almost forgotten, except by the specialist and the student, and it is no small part of this sketch to do them honor. The tiny spark of Faraday may be lost in the brilliancy of the million-candle-power search-light, yet the brilliancy of the search-light but enhances the wonder of the discovery of the spark.

The discovery of electro-magnetic induction marked the beginning of a new era; for in it lay all the possibilities of the future of electrical science. Michael Faraday, the third son of a poor English blacksmith, was born at Newington, Surrey, England, September 3, 1791. His father's health was never the best, and due to the resulting straitened circumstances his early education consisted of the merest rudiments of reading, writing and arithmetic. His early life was, no doubt, largely spent in the street; but at thirteen he became errand boy to a book-seller of London. About a year later he was apprenticed to a book binder, with whom he served seven years, learning the trade.

It was while an apprentice that Faraday began reading scientific articles on chemistry and physics in the books he was set to bind. He also tried to repeat the experiments of which he read. And more, he pondered over them long and earnestly, until he saw clearly the principles involved in them. It was in these early days of experimenting and self-education that the desire to become a philosopher was implanted in his mind. He embraced every chance for scientific study and caught every opportunity for intellectual self-improvement. In the last year of his apprenticeship he was enabled through the kindness of a customer at his master's shop, to attend a course of four lectures on chemistry, given by Sir Humphry Davy at the Royal Institution. This marked the turning point in his life. He made careful notes of the lecture, and afterward transcribed them neatly into a book and illustrated them with drawings of the apparatus used.

After completing his apprenticeship, Faraday began life as a journeyman bookbinder. He had, however, as he says, "no taste for trade." His love of science became a consuming desire that he sought in every way to gratify. Inspired by his longing for scientific pursuits, he sent his lecture notes to Sir Humphry Davy, with the request that if opportunity offered he would give him employment at the Royal Institution. Davy was favorably impressed with the lecture report, and sent a kindly reply to the young philosopher. Shortly after this a vacancy did happen to occur at the Institution, and upon the recommendation of Davy, Faraday was elected to the place. Thus, in 1813, in the humble capacity of an assistant charged with the simple duty of dusting and caring for the apparatus, Michael Faraday began the life that was destined to make him the first scientist of the world and to bring honor to the Institution which had given him his opportunity.

There is inspiration and encouragement to be found in reading the story of Faraday's success. He has been called a genius; but his genius seems to have largely consisted in persistent industry and the habit acquired in those early days of thinking over his experiments and reading until he had a clear perception of all there was in them. He lived in his work, and loved it. In the fifty busy years that followed his installment at the Royal Institution he digged deep into nature's secrets, and gave the world many brilliant gems as evidence of his industry. But of all his discoveries, *electro-magnetic induction* is the crowning masterpiece and that for which the world stands most his debtor.

The principle of conservation of energy, now so well known and universally accepted, was then but a vague guess in the minds of the more advanced in science. Faraday was among the first to accept the new doctrine, and many of his brilliant discoveries were made in his effort to prove the truth of these important generalizations. He was acquainted with Sturgeon's method of making magnets by sending a current of electricity through a wire wound around a bar of iron; and he reasoned, if electricity will make a magnet, a magnet ought to make electricity. As early as 1821 his note book contains this suggestion: "Convert magnetism into electricity." Again and again he attacked the problem; but it was not until the autumn of 1831 that his efforts to solve it were successful. Then in a series of experiments that have scarcely ever been equaled in brilliancy and originality, he gave to the world the principle on which is based the wonderful development of modern electrical science.

The principle is briefly stated. The space, around a wire carrying an electric current, or in the neighborhood of a magnet, has a directive effect upon a magnetic needle, and is hence called a magnetic field. Now if a conductor, or coil of wire, be placed in the field across the direction of a magnetic needle, and the field be varied either by varying the current or moving the magnet, a current will be developed in the conductor. It is impossible at this distance to appreciate the interest excited by the announcement of this principle, not only among scientists, but also among inventors and those who saw practical possibilities for the future; and probably no one more fully appreciated its value than Faraday himself. Yet he made no effort to develop it further, or even to protect his interest by a patent, as is common in these days. He was eminently a scientist, and this was his free gift to the world. He said: "I have rather been desirous of discovering new facts and relations than of exalting those already obtained, being assured the latter would find their full development hereafter."

Among the first to attempt successfully to exalt the new discovery was Pixii, an instrument maker of Paris, in 1832. He wound two coils of very fine insulated wire upon the ends of a piece of soft iron, bent in a horseshoe form. A permanent horseshoe magnet was then placed with poles very close to the ends of the iron in the coils. The field so produced was then rapidly varied by revolving the magnet on an axis parallel to its length. The soft iron cores of the coils became strongly magnetized as the poles of the revolving magnet came opposite to them; and their polarity was reversed at each half-revolution of the magnet. By this plan currents of considerable intensity and alternating in direction at each revolution were induced in the coil.

The ends of the coil were next connected to the external circuit through a "commutator." This is a device which is arranged to convert the alternating current of the coils into a current of one direction in the external circuit, and which in some form is found on all direct-current dynamos. Joseph Saxton, an American, improved upon Pixii's machine by rotating the coils, or armature as it is called, and making the heavier magnet stationary. The essential points of construction being worked out, improvements followed rapidly. Dr. Werner Siemans, of Berlin, introduced an important modification by making the revolving armature of a cylinder of soft iron, having a groove cut throughout its length on opposite sides. In these grooves a wire was wound and the armature was rotated on its axis between the poles of several magnets.

In all the earlier machines permanent magnets of steel were used. The next important step was to use electro-magnets of soft iron, excited by a current flowing through many turns of wire wound around the legs of the magnet. These could be made much more strongly magnetic than the permanent magnets. The exciting current was at first obtained from a small permanent magneto machine; but it was afterward found that the machine could be made self-exciting. Soft-iron electro-magnets, after being once magnetized, remain slightly magnetic. This will produce a weak current in the revolving armature which is turned into the magnet coils. The magnets are thus further magnetized, and again react upon the armature with greater intensity. In this way a *strong* current is rapidly built up, and after wholly or in part passing around the magnet coils to sustain its magnetism, can be carried out into the circuit to serve the great variety of purposes to which it is now put.

The essential points in the evolution of the dynamo can here be sketched only in broadest outline. Even to catalogue in detail, the improvements of Edison and Brush, Gramme and Wheatstone, and a host of others who have contributed to the work, would require a volume. One fact, however, should ever be kept in mind: Whatever may be the extent of the superstructure of electrical science, it is all built upon the foundation of electro-magnetic induction laid by Michael Faraday. The little "magnetic spark" he first produced, and the trembling of his galvanometer-needle, were but signals of the birth of the giant of the century.

These are the days of electricity and steel, and a fitting part of the intense age in which they exist. That we have as yet seen but a partial development of the possibilities of the electrical discovery, no one can doubt. The rush of the trolley car, and the blinding flash of the electric light, are but challenges thrown out to the future for even greater achievements. That they will come no one will question; but where is the daring prophet who will hazard a guess as to what they will be?

---

# THE UNKNOWN RAY AND ENTOGRAPHY

It is difficult to name the unknown. In the ancient world all the unknown was included in the idea of God. It remained for the evangelist to declare that God is a *spirit*—thus separating the natural forces of the material world from the Supreme Power who is from eternity.

This century has been the epoch of investigation into the nature of the imponderable forces. Sound and light and heat have been known as the principal agents of sensation since the first ages of man-life on the earth; but their nature has not been well understood until within the memories of men still living. Electricity was also vaguely known—but very indistinctly—from ancient times. It has remained for the scientific investigators of our age to enter into the secret parts of nature and lay bare to the understanding many of the hitherto unknown facts relating to the imponderable agents.

The laws of heat, of acoustics, of light, have been clearly arranged and taught; but they have not been placed beyond the reach of new interpretation and possibly not beyond the reach of complete revolution and reconstruction. That which has been accepted as definitely known with regard to these agents has now to be reviewed, and possibly to be learned over again from first principles.

As to electricity in its various forms and manifestations, that sublime and powerful agent began to be better known just before the middle of the century. Since that time there has been almost constant progress in the science of this great force, until at the present time it is handled, controlled and understood in its phenomena almost as easily as water is poured into a vessel, air compressed under a piston, or hydrogen made to inflate a balloon.

It has remained, however, for the last half decade of the great century to come upon and investigate a hitherto unknown force in nature. Certain it is that the new force exists, that it is everywhere, that it is a part of the profound agency by which life is administered, that its control is possible, and that its probable applications are as wonderful—perhaps more wonderful—than anything ever hitherto discovered by scientific investigation.

It is not unlikely that since the day, or evening, on which Galileo, with his little extemporized telescope, out in the garden of the Quirinal, at Rome, compelled bigotry to behold the shining horns of the crescent

Venus, thus opening as if by compulsion the sublime vista of the heavens and bringing in a new concept of the planetary and stellar worlds,—no such other discovery as that of the so-called Röntgen rays has been made. The results which seem likely to flow from this marvelous revelation surpass the human imagination. Let us try in a few words to realize the discovery, and define what it is.

It was on the eighth of November, 1895, that Dr. William Konrad Röntgen, of Würzburg, made the discovery which seems likely to contribute so much to our knowledge of the mysterious processes of nature. On that day Dr. Röntgen was working with a Crookes tube in his laboratory. This piece of apparatus is well known to students and partly known to general readers. It consists of a glass cylinder, elongated into tubular form, and hermetically closed at the ends. When the tube is made, the air is exhausted as nearly as possible from it, and the ends are sealed over a vacuum as perfect as science is able to produce. Through the two ends, bits of platinum wire are passed at the time of sealing, so that they project a little within and without. The interior of the tube is thus a vacuum into which at the two ends platinum wires extend. Electrical communication with outside apparatus is thus supplied.

It has long been known that on the discharge of an electrical current into this kind of vacuum peculiar and interesting phenomena are produced. The platinum wires at the two ends are connected with the positive and negative wires or terminals of an induction coil. When this is done, the electrical current discharged into the vacuum seems to flash out around the inner surfaces of the tube, in the form of light. There are brilliant coruscations from one end to the other of the tube. The tips of the platinum wire constituting the inner poles glow and seem to flame. That pole which is connected with the positive side of the battery is called the *anode*, or *upper* pole, and that which is connected with the negative, or receptive, side of the battery, is called the *cathode*, or lower pole. It was in his experimentation with this apparatus, and in particular in noticing the results at the cathode or lower end of the tube, that Professor Röntgen made his famous discovery. It was for this reason that the name of "cathode rays" has been given to the new radiant force; but Dr. Röntgen himself called the phenomena the X, or unknown, rays.

In the experimentation referred to, Röntgen had covered the glass tube at the end with a shield of black cardboard. This rendered the glow at the cathode pole completely invisible. It chanced that a piece of paper treated with platino-barium cyanide for photographic uses was on a bench near by. Notwithstanding the fact that the tube was covered with an opaque shield, so that no *light* could be transmitted, Professor Röntgen noticed that changes in the barium paper were taking place, *as though* it were exposed to the action of light! Black lines appeared on the paper, showing that the surface was undergoing chemical change from the action of some invisible and hitherto unknown force!

This was the moment of discovery. The philosopher began experimenting. He repeated what had been accidentally done and was immediately convinced that a force, or, as it were, invisible rays were streaming from the cathode pole of the tube through the glass, and through a substance absolutely opaque, and that these rays were performing their work at a distance on the surface of paper that was ordinarily sensitive only to the action of light.

Certain it was that *something* was doing this work. Certain it was that it was *not light.* Highly probable it was that it was not any form of *electricity*, for glass is impermeable to the electrical current. Certain it was that it was *not sound*, for there was no noise or atmospheric agitation to produce such a result. In a word, it was demonstrated then and there that a hitherto unknown, subtle and powerful agent had been discovered, the applications of which might be of almost infinite range and interest.

Professor Röntgen soon announced his discovery to the Physico-Medical Society of Würzburg. It was at the December meeting of this body that the new stage in human progress was declared. The news was soon flashed all over the world, and scientific men in every civilized country began at once to experiment with the cathode light—if light that might be called that lighted nothing.

In Röntgen's announcement he stated that there had been by the scientists Hertz and Lenard, in 1894, certain antecedent discoveries from which his own might in some sense be deduced. There was, however, a great difference between the discovery made by Röntgen and anything that had preceded it. His stage of progress in knowledge was this, that during the discharge of *one* kind of rays of force from the cathode pole in a Crookes tube *another kind* of rays are set free, which differ totally in their nature and effects from anything hitherto known. It is this fact which has indissolubly connected the name of Konrad Röntgen with that great bound in scientific knowledge which seems likely to modify nearly all the other scientific knowledge of mankind.

Everywhere, in the first months of 1896, the experimenters went to work to verify and apply the discovery of the German philosopher. It was at once discerned that the new force, since it would freely traverse opaque bodies and produce afterward chemical changes on sensitized surfaces similar to those ordinarily produced *by* light, might be used for delineating (we can hardly say *photo* graphing) the interior outlines and structure of opaque bodies!

On this line of experimentation the work at once began, and with remarkable success. Röntgen himself was the first man in the world to obtain, as *if* by photography, the invisible outline of objects through opaque materials. He soon obtained a delineation of the bones of a living hand through the flesh, which was only dimly traced in the resulting picture. In like manner coins were delineated through the leather of pocketbooks. Other objects were pictured through intervening plates of metal or boards of wood. The possibility of discovering the visible character of invisible things, and even *of seeing directly through* opaque materials into parts where neither light nor electricity can penetrate, was fully shown.

The work of picture taking in the interior of bodies and through opaque materials was quickly taken up by philosophers in England, France and the United States. Almost everywhere the physical laboratories witnessed daily this form of experimentation. Swinton, of London; Robb, of Trinity College, Dublin; Morton, of New York; Wright, of Yale University, and in particular Thomas A. Edison, of Menlo Park, attacked the new problem with scientific zeal, and with startling results. It remained for Edison to discover that the new force acted in some respects in the manner of *sound* rather than in the manner of *light*. Thus, for example, he showed that the invisible rays not only *pass through* substances that are opaque to light and non-conductors of electricity, but that the invisible rays *run around the edges and sides* of plates, then proceeding on their way somewhat in the manner of sound. A sound made on one side of a metallic plate is heard on the other side *partly* by transmission through the plate, and *partly* by going around the edges, by atmospheric transmission. The new force rays act in this manner, and Edison is said to have procured pictures by means of the invisible agent while it was *going around the corner* of an opaque obstruction!

The pre-eminence of Thomas A. Edison as a scientific explorer and inventor depends upon a quality of mind which enables him more easily than others—more distinctly than any others—to see the touch of each new discovery with existing conditions, and the application of it to the problems of life. Edison catches the premonitory spark struck in the darkness by some other master's hammer, and with that kindles a conflagration. Though not the discoverer of the Röntgen ray, he was able, as it would appear, to understand that discovery better even than the discoverer. He almost immediately applied the new increment of knowledge more successfully, we think, than any contemporary scientist. His experimentation led him directly to the discovery of the important fact that no photographic apparatus of any kind is needed to enable an observer to use the X-rays in the delineation or inspection of objects through opaque substances. He said within himself: "Why not pass the X-rays through the object to be inspected and then convert them into visibility, as if by fluorescence."

This scientific question Edison almost immediately solved. Fluorescence is a property which some transparent bodies have of producing, either on their surface or within their substance, light different in color from that of its origin. This happens, for example, when *green* crystals of fluor spar afford *blue* reflections of light. Glass may be rendered fluorescent, as is seen in the Geisler and Crookes tubes. Edison conceived the project of using this phenomenon to get back the invisible rays into visibility.

The substance which he employed was the tungstate of calcium. Taking crystals of this chemical compound, he spread the same over a cloth or paper screen, and used that screen to catch and convert the invisible images carried against it by the X-rays. To his surprise, his experiment was completely successful. All that is needed in this case is the cathode light, the object to be examined (as for instance the hand), and the screen treated with tungstate of calcium. The observer looks through the screen, or into it, and sees *with the unaided eye* the invisible interior parts of the object examined, held between the screen and the cathode light. The invisible rays take the image of the interior parts of an opaque object, and carry that image to the screen, where it is reconverted into visibility and delivered to the eye of the observer, without the aid of any instrument at all! It is on this simple principle that Edison has invented his surgical and physiological lamp. The announcement is that with this lamp the surgeon may look through the calcium tungstate screen and examine, for example, the fractured bones of the hand, and set them perfectly by actual inspection of the parts with his eye!

What then *is* the cathode ray? At the present time its nature is not understood. That it is a form or mode of motion goes with the saying—unless it should be presently shown that all the imponderable forces are really *material* in their nature; that is, that they are an inconceivably fine and attenuated form of matter in varying manifestations.

The cathode rays are not light. They are not sound. They are not electricity or magnetism. They are not heat. They are not any of the known forms of force. They seem to be a new transformation of some one or more of the known agents. It has long been observed that *motion* is accompanied with *sound*, and that motion also, if increased, becomes manifest in *heat*. It is known that heat is convertible into light, and light into electricity.

It is possible that at the bottom of all these phenomena lies the force of gravitation. This force is absolute and universal. All the others are partial and limited. All the others, even the newly discovered cathode rays, are subject to obstruction by certain forms of matter; that is, to them certain forms of matter are opaque. But gravitation knows no opacity in the universe. No atom of matter is exempt from its sway. It streams through all obstructive media as though such media did not exist. It would appear that heat, light, electricity, sound, the cathode rays, and all other forms of force in nature are probably variations, and as it were limited expressions and manifestations, of *the one supreme force* that supports the constitution of the physical universe; and that one supreme force is *gravitation*!

---

# Stages in Biological Inquiry

# THE NEW INOCULATION

Any account of the scientific progress of this century which omits the name of Louis Pasteur would be lamentably incomplete. In that part of science which relates strictly to human life and the means of preserving it, the work of this great man must be placed in the first rank. Indeed, we believe that no other stride in biological investigation from the beginning of time has been so great in its immediate and prospective results as has been the increment contributed by Pasteur and his contemporary Koch. The success of these two experimental philosophers grew out of the substitution of a new theory for one that had hitherto prevailed respecting some of the fundamental processes in living matter.

Up to about the close of the third quarter of this century, the belief continued to prevail in the possibility of the propagation and production of germ life without other germ life to precede it. It was held that fermentation is not dependent upon living organisms, and that fermentation may be excited in substances from which all living germs have been excluded. This belief led to the theory of *abiogenesis* so-called—a term signifying the production of life without life to begin with.

The question involved in this theory was hotly debated by philosophers and scientists in the Sixties and Seventies. The first great work of Pasteur in biological investigation was his successful demonstration of the impossibility of spontaneous generation. About 1870, he became a careful experimenter with the phenomena of fermentation. As his work proceeded, he was more convinced that fermentation can never occur in the absence and exclusion of living germs; and this view of the deep-down processes in living matter has now been accepted as correct.

The next stage in the work of Pasteur was the discovery that certain substances, such as glycerine, are products of fermentation. From this foundation firmly established he passed on to consider the phenomena of disease. He had been, in the first place, a teacher in a normal school at Paris. In 1863, when he was thirty-nine years of age, he was a professor of geology. Afterward he had a chair of chemistry at the Sorbonne. In 1856 we find him experimenting with light, and after that he turned to biological investigations. This led him to the results mentioned above, and presently to the discovery that the contagious and infectious diseases with which men and the lower animals are affected are in general the results of processes in the system that are nearly analagous to fermentation, and that such diseases are therefore traceable ultimately to the existence of living germs.

This view of the case brought Pasteur to a large and general investigation of bacteria. The bacterium may be defined as a microscopic vegetable organism; or it may be called an *animal* organism; for in the deep-down life of germs there is not much difference between vegetable and animal—perhaps no difference at all. The bacterium is generally a jointed rod-like filament of living matter, and its native world seems to be any putrefying organic substance.

Bacteria are the smallest of microscopic organisms. They are widely diffused in the natural world, existing independently and also in a parasitical way, in connection with larger forms of organic life. They multiply with the greatest rapidity. On the whole, the bacterium fulfills its vital offices in two ways, or with two results; first, *fermentation*, and secondly, *disease*.

To this field of inquiry Pasteur devoted himself with the greatest assiduity. He began to investigate the diseased tissue of animals, and was rewarded with the discovery of the germs from which the disease had come. It was found that the bacteria of one disease are different from those of another disease, or in a word that the microscopic organisms which produce morbid conditions in animals are differentiated into genera and species and varieties, in the same manner as are the animals, birds and fishes, of the world. A new realm of life invisible save by the aid of the microscope, began to be explored, and practical results began to follow.

Pasteur at length announced his ability to *produce* infectious diseases by inoculation; and of this his proofs and demonstrations, were complete. In the next place he announced his ability to *counteract* the ravages, of certain classes of diseases (those called zymotic) by inoculating the animal suffering therefrom with what he called an "attenuated" or "domesticated" virus of the given disease.

The matter first came to a practical issue by the inoculation of well animals with the attenuated virus. The animals so treated became *immune*; that is, exempt from the infection of the given disease. Pasteur gave public demonstrations in the fields near Paris, using the disease called splenic fever, and sheep as the subjects of his experimentation. The whole civilized world was astonished with the results. The tests were conducted in such a way as to preclude the possibility of error. It was shown, in a word, that by the simple process of inoculating well animals with the modified poison the infectious disease might be avoided.

It were long to tell the story of the experimentation and discovery that now followed. The last quarter of the century has been fruitful in the greatest results. The bacilli of one disease after another have been discovered, and the means have been invented of defending the larger animal life from the ravages of microscopic organisms.

But what is an "attenuated" virus? Pasteur and other scientists have shown that by the inoculation of suitable material, such as a piece of flesh, with the poison of a given disease, the bacteria on which that disease depends rapidly multiply and diffuse themselves through the substance. If poison be taken from the *first* body of infected material and carried to *another*, that other becomes infected; and from that the third; from the third the fourth, and so on to the tenth generation.

It was noticed, however, that with each transference of the virus to a new organic body the bacilli were modified somewhat in form and activity. They became, so to speak, less savage. The bacterium which at the beginning had been for its savagery a wolf, became in the second body a cur; then a hound; then a spaniel; and then a diminutive lapdog! The bacteria were thus said to be "domesticated;" for the process was similar to the domestication of wild animals into tame. The virus was said to be "attenuated;" that is, made thin or fine; that is, its poisonous and death-dealing quality, was so reduced as to make it comparatively innocuous.

If after the process of attenuation was complete—if after the bacteria were once thoroughly domesticated and the poison produced by them be then introduced into a well subject, that subject would indeed become diseased, but so mildly diseased as scarcely to be diseased at all. In such a case the result was of a kind to be called in popular language a mere "touch" of the disease. In such case the severe ravages of the malady would be prevented; but the subject would be rendered incapable of taking the disease a second time.

On this line of fact and theory Pasteur successfully pressed his work. One disease after another was investigated. It was demonstrated in the case of both the lower animals and men that a large number of maladies and plagues might be completely disarmed of their terrors by the process of inoculation. The name of Pasteur became more and more famous. The celebrated Pasteur Institute was founded at Paris, under the patronage of the French Government, and in some sense under the patronage of the whole world. To this establishment diseased subjects were taken for treatment, and here experimentation was carried on over a wide range of facts.

The value of the results attained can hardly be overestimated. The fear which mankind have long entertained on account of plagues and epidemics, and the loss which the animal industries of the world have sustained, were largely abated. As yet the use of the Pasteur methods for the prevention and cure of disease is by no means universal; but the knowledge which has come of his investigations and of the results of them has diffused itself among all civilized nations, and the hygienic condition of almost every community has been most favorably affected by the new knowledge which we possess of bacteria and of the means of destroying them.

Pasteur, whose recent death has been mourned by the best part of mankind, was an explorer and forerunner. His industry in his chosen field of investigation was prodigious. When he was already nearly seventy years of age, he undertook the investigation of hydrophobia, with the purpose of discovering, if he might, the germ of that dreaded disease, thus preparing a method for inoculation against it.

Hydrophobia is one of the most subtle diseases ever known. So obscure and uncertain are its phenomena that many able men have been led to doubt the *existence* of such a disease! The mythological origin of the malady in the supposed influence of a dog-star seemed to strengthen the view that hydrophobia, as a specific disease, does not exist. It is undeniably true that the great majority of the cases of so-called rabies are pure myths. Under investigation they melt away into nothing but alarm and fiction. However, there appeared to be a residue of actual hydrophobia, though the disease as tested by its name exists in fancy rather than fact.

In any event, Pasteur began to investigate hydrophobia, and at length discovered the bacilli which produce it. At least he found in animals affected with rabies, notably in the spinal marrow of such animals, minute living organisms, having the form of thread-like animalculæ, with heads at one end. The microscope showed also among these thread-like bodies other organisms that were like small circular black specks, or disks.

The next step in the work was to test the result by inoculating a well animal with these bodies. Pasteur selected rabbits for his experimentation. When the experiment was made, the inoculated rabbit was presently attacked with the disease, and soon died in spasms. The repetition of the experiment was attended with like results.

The philosopher next tried his established method of domesticating, or attenuating, the poison. The spinal cord of a rabid dog was obtained, and with this the first rabbit was inoculated. In about two weeks it took hydrophobia. Hereupon the spinal cord was extracted, and the second rabbit was inoculated; then the third; then the fourth, and so on. It was observed, however, that at each stage the intensity of the disease was in this way strangely increased; but the period of inoculation became shorter and shorter.

It was next found that by preserving the spinal cords of the animals that had died of the disease—by preserving them in dry tubes—the poison gradually lost its power. At last the virus seemed to die altogether. Then the experiment of inoculating against the disease was begun. A dog was first inoculated with dead virus. No result followed. Then he was inoculated with stale virus, and then with other virus not so stale. It was found that by continuing this process the animal might be rendered wholly insusceptible to the disease.

The next step was the human stage of experimentation. It was in July of 1885 that Pasteur first employed his method on a human subject. A boy had been bitten and lacerated by a rabid dog. The inoculation was thought to prove successful. Soon afterward some bitten children were taken from the United States to Paris, and were treated against the expected appearance of hydrophobia. Others came from different parts of the continent. Within fourteen months more than two thousand five hundred subjects were treated, and it is claimed that the mortality from hydrophobia was reduced to a small per cent of what it had been before.

It should be said, however, that neither have the results arrived at by Pasteur respecting the character of rabies been so clear, nor have his experiments on subjects supposed to be poisoned with the disease been so successful as in the case of other maladies. It remains, nevertheless, to award to Louis Pasteur *the first rank* among the bacteriologists of our day, as well as a first place among the philanthropists of the century. Only Robert Koch, of Germany, is to be classed in the same list with him.

# KOCH'S BATTLE WITH THE INVISIBLE ENEMY

There was a great *negative* reason for the success of the World's Columbian Exposition. The cholera did NOT come! It is quite true that there is no *if* in history; but IF the cholera had come, IF the plague had broken out in our imperial Chicago, what would have become of the Columbian Exposition? Certainly the Man of Genoa would have had to seek elsewhere for a great international gathering in his honor.

The cholera did not arrive, although it was expected. The antecedent conditions of its coming were all present; but it came not. The American millions discerned that the dreaded plague was at bay; a feeling of security and confidence prevailed; the summer of 1893 went by, and not a single case of Asiatic cholera appeared west of the Alleghenies. We are not sure that a single case appeared on the mainland of North America. And why not?

It was because the increasing knowledge of mankind, reinforced with philanthropy and courage, had drawn a line north and south across Western Europe, and had said, *Thus far and no farther*. Indeed, there were several lines drawn. The movement of cholera westward from the Orient began to be obstructed even before it reached Germany. It was obstructed in Italy. It was obstructed seriously on the meridian of the Rhine. It was obstructed almost finally at the meridian of London. It was completely and gloriously obstructed at the harbor of New York.

Civilization has never appeared to a better advantage than in the building of her defences against the westward invasion of cholera. There have been times within two decades of the present when in the countries east of the Red Sea 3000 people have died daily of the Asiatic plague. Egypt has been ravaged. The ports of the Mediterranean have been successfully invaded. Commerce, reckless of everything except her own interests, has taken the infection on shipboard, and sailed with it to foreign lands, as though it were a precious cargo! Importers, anxious for merchandise, have stood ready to receive the plague, and plant it without regard to consequences. But in the midst of all this, a new power has arisen in the world, and standing with face to the east, has drawn a sword, before the circle of which even the spectral shadow of cholera has quailed and gone back! Humanity might well break out in rhapsody and jubilee over this great victory.

Among the personal agencies by which cholera has been excluded from Europe and America, first and greatest is Dr. Robert Koch, of Berlin. He, more than any other one man, has contributed to the glorious exemption. Dr. Koch, now by the favor of his Emperor, Baron Koch, is one of those heroic spirits who go before the human race exploring the route, casting up a highway and gathering out the stones. Thus shall the feet of the oncoming millions be not bruised and their shouts of joy be not turned to lamentation.

Robert Koch was born at Klausthal, in the Hartz mountains, on the eleventh of December, 1843. He is a German of the Germans. In his youth he was a student of medicine at Göttingen, where at the age of twenty-three he took his first degree. He was by nature and from his boyhood a devotee of science. For about ten years he practiced his profession, but continued his studies with indefatigable zeal. The investigations of Pasteur had already filled Europe with applause when Koch, following on the same lines of scientific exploration, began to enlarge the borders of knowledge. He became a bacteriologist of the first rank. He began to investigate the causes and nature of contagion; but as late as 1876 his name was still unknown in the cyclopædias.

Koch was twenty-one years the junior of Pasteur; but his enthusiasm and genius now bore him rapidly to a fame as great as that of his predecessor. His first remarkable achievement was a demonstration of the cause and cure of splenic fever in cattle. He showed, just as Pasteur had done in similar cases, that the plague in question was due to the specific poison of a bacterium, and that the disease might be cured by inoculation against it. This he proceeded to do, and the demonstration and good work brought him to the attention of the old Emperor. Dr. Koch was made a member of the Imperial Board of Health in Berlin.

A greater discovery was already at the door. Dr. Koch began a careful investigation into the nature of consumption. His discovery of the germ of splenic fever, and that of chicken cholera, as well as the general results in this direction in other laboratories of Europe, led him to the conjecture that consumption also is a zymotic or bacterial disease. His inquiry into this subject began in 1879, and extended to March of 1882. On that day, in a paper before the Physiological Society of Berlin, he announced the discovery of the *tubercle bacillus*. He was able to demonstrate the existence of the germ of consumption, and to describe its methods of life, as well as the character of his ravages.

Here then at last was laid bare the true origin of the most fatal disease which has ever afflicted mankind. He who has not informed himself with respect to the almost universal prevalence of consumption among the nations of the earth, or taken note of the mortality from that dreaded enemy, by which nearly one-sixth of the human race sooner or later perishes, will not have realized the awful character of this enemy. To attack such a foe, to force him into a corner, even as Siegfried did the Grendel in his cavern, was an achievement of which the greatest of mankind might well be proud.

The discovery of the bacillus of consumption by no means assured the cure of the disease; but it foretokened the time when a cure would be found. This prophecy, though it has not yet been clearly fulfilled, is, in the closing years of the century, in process of fulfillment. The enemy does not readily yield; but such has been the gain in the contest that already within the last twenty years the mortality from consumption of the lungs has fallen off more than forty per cent! Much of this gain has been made by the reviving confidence of human beings that sooner or later tuberculosis would be destroyed. Hygiene has done its part; and other circumstances have conduced to the same result. Though neither Dr. Koch nor any other man living has been able as yet positively to meet and vanquish consumption in open battle, yet the goblin has in a measure been robbed of his terrors. He is no longer boastful and victorious over the human race.

After the discovery of the tubercle bacillus, the fame of Robert Koch became world-wide. In the following year he was made a privy councilor, and was placed in charge of an expedition organized by the German government to go into Egypt and India for the investigation of the causes of Asiatic cholera. The expedition was engaged in this work for nearly a year. Koch pursued his usual careful method of scientific experimentation. He exposed himself to the contagion of cholera, but his science and fine constitution stood him well in hand, and he returned unharmed.

It was in May of 1884 that he was able to announce the discovery of the *coma bacillus*, that is, the bacterium of cholera. Here, again he had the enemy at bay. For long ages the Asiatic plague had ravaged the countries of the East with little hindrance to its spread or fatality. The disease would appear as an epidemic at intervals and sweep all before it. The wave of death would roll on westward from country to country, until it would subside, as if by exhaustion, in the far west. Two or three times within the century cholera had been fatally scattered through American cities. It had spread westward along the rivers of the Ohio and Mississippi valleys, and into country districts, where villages and hamlets were decimated.

The discovery of Koch was a virtual proclamation that this ruin of mankind from the Asiatic plague should cease. The knowledge that the disease was due to a living bacterium, that without the germ and the spread of the germ the plague could not exist, was a virtual announcement that in the civilized countries it should *not* any longer exist.

The discoverer was now set high in the estimation of mankind. Imperial Germany best of all countries rewards its benefactors. France is fascinated with adventure; Great Britain with slaughter; America with bare political battles; but Germany sees the true thing, and rewards it. Koch was immediately placed beyond want by his government, and titles and honors came without stint.

The Empire would fain have such a man at the seat of power. Dr. Koch was, in 1885, made a professor in the University of Berlin. The new chair of Hygiene was created for him, and he was made Director of the Hygienic Institute. It was in this capacity that armed with influence and authority and having the resources of the government virtually at his disposal, he directed in the great scientific work by which a bulwark against cholera was drawn almost literally across Europe, and was defended as if with the mounted soldiery of science and humanity. True enough, cholera managed to plant itself in Italy in 1886, and in Hamburg in 1892, and the plague was scattered into several German towns. But it came to Hamburg by water, not by land. It did there during the summer a dreadful work, but the battle was the Waterloo of the enemy. Not again while the present order continues will it be possible for the dreaded epidemic to get the mastery of a great German city.

It was to be anticipated that Dr. Koch's discovery of the tubercle bacillus would lead him on to the discovery of a cure for tuberculosis. Very naturally his thought on this subject was borne in the direction of inoculation. That method had been used by Pasteur and by himself in the case of other infectious diseases. Why should it not be employed in consumption? If the "domestication," so-called, of the virus of splenic fever and the use of the modified poison as an antiseptic preventive of the disease was successful, as it had been proved to be, why should this not be done with the attenuated virus of consumption?

The last five years of the ninth decade were spent by Dr. Koch in experimentation on this subject. He found that the tubercular poison might be treated in the same manner as the poison of other infectious diseases. He experimented with methods for domesticating the bacillus of consumption, and reached successful results. On the fourteenth of November, 1890, he published in a German medical magazine at Berlin a communication on a possible remedy for tuberculosis. He had prepared a sort of lymph suitable for hypodermic injection, and with this had experimented on a form of *external* tuberculosis called lupus. This disease is a consumption of the skin and adjacent tissues. It is a malady almost as dreadful as consumption of the lungs, but is by no means frequent in its occurrence. It is found only at rare intervals by the medical practitioner.

Dr. Koch had demonstrated that lupus is a true tuberculosis—that the germ which produces it is the same bacillus which produces consumption of the lungs. He accordingly directed his effort to cases of lupus, treating the patients with hypodermic injections which he had prepared from the modified form of the tubercular poison. He was successful in the treatment, and was able to announce, to the joy of the world, that he had discovered a cure for lupus; and the announcement went so far as to express a belief in the salutary character of the remedy in the treatment of consumption of the lungs.

Dr. Koch, however, with the usual caution of the true men of science, did not announce his tuberculin, or lymph, as a cure for pulmonary consumption. He did not even declare that it was positively a remedy for the other forms of tuberculosis, but did announce his cure of cases of lupus by the agent which he had prepared. The world, after its manner, leaped at conclusions, and the newspapers of two continents, in their usual office of disseminating ignorance, trumpeted Koch's discovery as the end of tubercular consumption.

In January of 1891, Dr. Koch published to the world the composition of his remedy. It consists of a glycerine extract prepared by the cultivation of tubercle bacilli. The lymph contains, as it were, the poisonous matter resulting from the life and activity of the tubercle bacterium. The fluid is used by hypodermic injection, and when so administered produces both a general and local reaction. The system is powerfully affected. A sense of weariness comes on. The breathing is labored. Nausea ensues; and a fever supervenes which lasts for twelve or fifteen hours. It is now known that the action of the remedy is not directly against the tubercle bacilli, but rather against the affected tissue in which they exist. This tissue is destroyed and thrown off by the agency of the lymph; being destroyed, it is eliminated and cast out, carrying with it the bacteria on which the disease depends.

The results which have followed the administration of Koch's lymph for consumption of the lungs have not met the expectation of the public; but something has been accomplished. Ignorant enthusiasm has meanwhile subsided, and scientific men in both Europe and America are pressing the inquiry in a way which promises in due time the happiest results.

# ACHIEVEMENTS IN SURGERY

It will not do to disparage the work of the ancients. The old world, long since fallen below the horizon of the past, had races of men and individuals who might well be compared with the greatest of to-day. In a general way, the ancients were great as thinkers and weak as scientists. They were great in the fine arts and weak in the practical arts. This is true of the Hindus, the Egyptians, the Greeks, the Romans, even of the Aztecs and the Peruvians.

The art work of these old peoples, whether in sculpture, painting or poetry, surpassed, if it did not eclipse, corresponding periods of modern times. In some of the practical arts the old races were proficient. In architecture, which combines the æsthetic and practical elements, the man of antiquity was at least the equal of the man of the present. In one particular art—a sort of humanitarian profession based on natural science and directed to the preservation of life—the ancients had a measure of proficiency. This art was surgery. The surgeon was even from the beginning, and he will no doubt be even to the end.

The great advance which has been made in surgical science and practice is shown in two ways: first, in a great increase of courage, by which the surgeon has been led on to the performance of operations that were hitherto considered rash, audacious or impossible; and secondly, by the immunity which the surgeon has gained in the treatment of wounds through the increased knowledge he possesses of putrefaction and the means of preventing it. It were hard to say whether the surgeon's increase of skill and courage in performing operations has equalled his increased skill in the after treatment of wounds.

These improvements have all proceeded from scientific investigation. They have come of the application of scientific methods to the treatment of surgical diseases. With the investigations of Pasteur and the development of the science of bacteriology, it was seen at a glance how large an influence such investigation must have in the work of the surgeon. The publication of Tyndall's "Essays on the Floating Matter of the Air in Relation to Putrefaction and Infection," in 1881, gave a great impulse to the new practice; but that practice had been already confirmed by the great and original work of Sir Joseph Lister, an English surgeon who as early as 1860 had introduced the antiseptic method of bandaging.

It is within the last forty years that the greatest marvels of modern surgery have been performed. It would seem that no part of the human body is now beyond the reach of surgical remedy. Almost every year has witnessed some new and daring invasion of the fortress of life with a view to saving it. Old opinions with respect to what parts of the human economy are really vital have been abolished; and a new concept of the relation of life to organism has prevailed.

Until recently it was supposed that the peritoneal cavity and the organs contained therein, such as the stomach, the liver, the bowels, etc., could not be entered by the surgeon without the certain result of death. To do so at the present time is the daily experience in almost every great hospital. The complexity of civilization has inflicted all manner of hurts on the human body, and the malignity of disease has spared no part. It was supposed that the cranial cavity could not be entered or repaired without producing fatal results. It was taken for granted that certain organs could not be touched, much less treated capitally, without destroying the subject's life. But one exploration has followed another and one successful adventure has been succeeded by another still more successful until the surgeon's work is at the present time performed within a sphere that was until recently supposed to be entirely beyond his reach.

As to the liver, that great organ is freely examined and is treated surgically with considerable freedom. This is true also of the stomach, which until recently was supposed to be entirely beyond the surgeon's touch. Within the last two decades sections of the stomach have been made and parts of the organ removed. Not a few cases are recorded in which subjects have fully recovered after the removal of a part of the stomach. Sections of the intestinal canal have also been made with entire success. Several inches of that organ have in some cases been entirely removed, with the result of recovery! The spleen has been many times removed; but it has been recently noted that a decline in health and probably death at a not distant date generally follow this operation.

The disease called appendicitis has either in our times become wonderfully frequent or else the improved methods of diagnosis have made us acquainted with what has long been one of the principal maladies of mankind. The *appendix vermiformis* seems to be a useless remnant of anatomical structure transmitted to us from a lower animal condition. At least such is the interpretation which scientists generally give to this hurtful and dangerous tube-like blind channel in connection with the bowels. That it becomes easily inflamed and is the occasion of great loss of life can not be doubted. Its removal by surgical operation is now regarded as a simple process which even the unlearned surgeon, if he be careful and talented, may safely perform. The surgical treatment of appendicitis has become so common as to attract little or no notice from the profession. Even the country neighborhood no longer regards such a piece of surgery as sensational.

The use of surgical means in the cure, that is the removal, of tumors, both external and internal, has been greatly extended and perfected. The surgeon now carries a quick eye for the tumor and a quick remedy for it. In nearly all cases in which it has not become constitutional he effects a speedy cure with the knife. The cancerous part is cut away. It has been observed that as the recent mortality from consumption has decreased cancerous diseases have become more frequently fatal. Whether or not there be anything vicarious in the action of these two great maladies we know not; but statistics show that since the beginning of Pasteur's discoveries the one disease has diminished and the other increased in almost a corresponding ratio. Meanwhile, however, surgery has opposed itself not only to cancers but to all kinds of tumors, until danger from these sores has been greatly lessened. The removal of internal tumors such as the ovarian, is no longer, except in complicated and neglected cases, a matter of serious import. Such work is performed in almost every country town, and the amount of human life thus rescued from impending death is very great. The work of lithotomy is not any longer regarded with the dread which formerly attended it. In fact, every kind of disease and injury which in its own nature is subject to surgical remedy has been disarmed of its terror. The eye and the ear and all of the more delicate organs have become subject to repair and amendment to a degree that may well excite wonder and gratify philanthropy.

But it is not only in the actual processes of surgery that this great improvement in human art may be noted. The treatment of wounds with respect to their cure by preserving them from bacterial and other poisons has been so greatly improved that it is now regarded almost as a crime to permit suppuration and other horrible processes which were formerly supposed to be the necessary concomitants of healing. The hospital, whether military or civil, was formerly a scene that might well horrify and make sick a visitant. It was putrefaction everywhere. It was stench and poisonous effluvia. The conditions were such as to make sick if not destroy even those who were well. How then could the injured sufferers escape?

It is one of the crowning glories of our time that no such scene now exists in any civilized country. No such will ever exist again, unless science should lose its grip on the human mind and the civilized life subside into barbarism. The surgeon would now be held in ill-repute that should permit to any considerable degree the processes of putrefaction to take place in a wound of which he has had the care. The introduction of antiseptic and aseptic methods has made him a master in this respect. The skillful surgeon bids defiance to the microbes that hover in swarming millions ravenous for admission to every hurt done to the human body. To them a wound is a festival. To them a sore is a royal banquet to which through the invisible realm a proclamation goes forth, "Come ye! Come to the banquet which death is preparing out of life!" All this the modern surgeon disappoints with a smile and a wave of his hand. The invisible swarms of invading animalculæ are swept back. Not a single bacterium can any longer enter the most inviting wound while the surgeon stands ready with drawn sword to defend the portals of life.

---

# Great Religious Movements

# Defence on New Lines

In a period so intensely active and progressive as the nineteenth century has been, in politics, science and literature, it would have been surprising if the church had remained inert, wrapped like a mummy in the cerements of the past. At the beginning of the century, there were voices on all hands loudly proclaiming that it was dead; that it was antiquated and obsolete; that it had lost touch with the life of the time, that it was a relic of exploded superstition; and as a great writer said, had fallen into a godless mechanical condition, standing as the lifeless form of a church, a mere case of theories, like the carcass of a once swift camel, left withering in the thirst of the universal desert. That in certain circles there was ground for such reproach is sufficiently proved. Materialism had crept into its colleges, sapping away their spiritual life and driving young men either into Atheism or into the Roman Catholic Communion. Such activity as it had, was in the evangelical circles only The common people still listened eagerly to Wesley's successors and were intensely in earnest in the Christian life and work. It was at the top that the tree was dying, where the currents of the philosophy of Voltaire struck the branches, and where Hume's scorching radicalism blighted its leaves. In the universities, and the clubs, not in the workshops, was religion scorned and contemned.

There was soon, however, to be a quickening of the dry bones. The spirit of the time—the zeit-geist—began to move in the Church. It was the spirit of investigation, of scientific inquiry, of rigorous test. The older preachers and religious authorities still droned about the duty of defending the faith "once for all" delivered to the saints. In spite of their protests, the younger men would go down into the crypt of the Church, and examine the foundations of the building. They could not be kept back by authoritative assurances that the stones were sound, and were well and truly laid. The hysterical protests against the irreverence of examination fell on deaf ears. The answer was the simple insistance on investigation. The very reluctance to permit it was an indication that it would not bear investigation.

At the opening of the century, this idea, expressed in varying forms, was rapidly becoming prevalent. The citadel of the Church was assaulted, by some with ferocity, and by others with scorn and contempt. The defence was on the old lines of denunciation of the wickedness of the assailants, of vituperative epithets, and of the assumption of special and divine illumination. The issue of the conflict would not have been doubtful, had it been continued with these tactics. The Church would have been relegated to the limbo of superstition and the hide-bound pedantry of ecclesiasticism, if new defenders on new principles had not entered the lists. Reinforcement came from a band of philosophic thinkers of whom Wordsworth and Coleridge were the pioneers. The influence of both these men was underestimated at the time. They appeared weak and ineffective, but the ideas to which they gave expression, entered the minds of stronger men, who applied them with more vigorous force. The Church, Coleridge declared, as Carlyle interprets him, was not dead, but tragically, asleep only. It might be aroused and might again become useful, if only the right paths were opened. Coleridge could not open the paths, he could but vaguely show the depth and volume of the forces pent up in the Church; but he insisted that they were there, that eternal truth was in Christianity, and that out of it must come the light and life of the world. As his little band of hearers listened to him, they saw the first faint gleams of the light which was to illumine the world and make the darkness and degradation of the materialistic philosophy an impossibility to the devout mind. Thus he stood at the beginning of the nineteenth century, as Erasmus stood at the beginning of the sixteenth, perceiving and proclaiming the existence of truths which others were to apply to the needs of the time.

To ascertain precisely in what form the forces of Christianity existed and how they might be applied to nineteenth century life, became early in the nineteenth century the problem on which the best thought of the time was concentrated. Coleridge's unshaken conviction that it was solvable, inspired many with courage. Whately, Arnold, Schleiermacher, Bunsen, Ewald, Newman, Hare, Milman, Thirlwall and many others, approached it from different directions. The spirit of scientific investigation that was in the air was applied with reverent hands, but with unsparing resolve to ascertain the exact truth. The investigation was no longer confined to dogma; a proof text from the Bible was no longer sufficient to close a controversy. The Bible itself must be subjected to investigation. This was indeed going to the foundations. There was a wild outcry against rationalism and iconoclasm, but the search for truth and fact went on. As in a siege, the garrison must sometimes destroy with their own hands outworks which cannot be successfully defended, and may be made a vantage ground for the enemy, so the defenders of Christianity set themselves to the task of finding out how much of the current theology was credible and tenable, and how much might wisely be abandoned, to insure the safety of the remainder. The discoveries of Geology, Astronomy and of Biology could not be denied, yet their testimony was contrary to Christian doctrine. "The world was made in six natural days," said the old Christian preacher. "The world was thousands of years in the making," said the geologist. The preacher appealed to his Bible, the geologist appealed to the rocks. The issue was fairly joined, and in the early years of the century it seemed as if there was no alternative but that of believing the Bible and denying science, or believing science and giving up the Bible; it seemed impossible to believe both. When the scientific theologian ventured to suggest that the word "day," might mean age, or period, there was another outcry that the Bible was being surrendered to the enemy. But it was realized that the message of the Bible to the world was not scientific, and that its usefulness was not impaired by the suggested mode of understanding its record of creation; and gradually the surrender was accepted. It is true that to this day there are some who will not accept it, as there is at least one preacher who insists, on the authority of the Bible, that "the sun do move," but the number diminishes in every generation. A beginning was made in attaining the true view of the Bible which led further and has not yet reached its limits. Having admitted that the Bible was not given to teach science the Church has to decide whether it can admit the theory of evolution and whether its records of history are authoritative. These questions are so fundamental that the strife of Calvinism and Arminianism and the question of the double procession of the Holy Spirit, which seemed vital to our fathers have faded into relative insignificance.

# Evangelical Activity

While these storms were agitating the upper air, and the thunderous echoes reverberated through the mountains, the work on the plain went rapidly forward. However the scholars and the theologians might decide the questions at issue between them, the working forces were profoundly convinced that the Gospel was the great need of the world, and they put out new energy and applied all the powers of the mind to devising new methods for its propagation. The increased facilities of travel, the improved means of communication and, above all, the power of the printing-press, were all seized and harnessed to service in the dissemination of the Gospel. No characteristic of this century is so prominent as this intense activity and aggressive energy. From every secular movement, the church has taken suggestions for its own advancement. Trade-unionism has suggested Christian Endeavor and the Evangelical Alliance; the public school system has developed the International Lesson system in the Sunday School; the political convention has taught the advantages of great religious conferences; the principles of military organization have been utilized in the Salvation Army. If in some circles religion seems to have been a fight over doctrines and theories, in others it has seemed a ceaseless, untiring struggle for converts. In no century since the first century of the Christian era has the zeal of propagation, with no element of proselytism in it, taken so strong a hold of the followers of Christ. To translate the Bible into every tongue, to carry the Gospel message to every people, and to evangelize the masses at home, prodigious efforts have been put forth, and enormous sums of money have been expended. Mental activity, uncompromising veracity, indefatigable energy, have characterized the Church through the century, and its closing years show no abatement in any of these characteristics. A brief sketch of some of the more prominent of these developments can render the fact only more, obvious.

# Bible Revision

One of the most important events of the century to the English speaking world is the Revision of the Bible. Its full effect is not yet felt, as the book which was the product of the Revisers' labors is but slowly winning its way into use in the Church and the home. Like its predecessor, the Authorized Version now in general use, it has to encounter the prejudice which comes from long familiarity with the book in use and from the veneration for the phraseology in which the precious truths, are expressed. Yet from the beginning of the century the need of an improved translation was felt and several persons, undertook to supply it, but with very objectionable results. The principal bases of the need were serious. One was that many words and phrases have in the nineteenth century a meaning entirely different from the one they had in the early part of the seventeenth century when the Authorized Version was issued. One case in point is Mark vi. 22, in which Salome asks that the head of John the Baptist be given her "by and by in a charger." In 1611 the expression by and by meant immediately or forthwith, and was a correct translation, while with us it means a somewhat indefinite future and is therefore an incorrect translation. With the noun, too, the meaning has changed. Our idea of a charger is of a war-horse, not of a dish, which the original conveys. A second reason for the revision was that there were in the libraries in this century several manuscripts of the original, much older than those to which the translators of the Authorized Version had access when they undertook their work. A third reason was that a notable advance had been made in scholarship in the interval, and learned men were much better acquainted with the Hebrew and Greek idiom than were any of the scholars of the King James period. For these three, among other reasons, a revision was necessary, that the unlearned reader might have, as nearly as was possible, the exact equivalent in English of the words of the Bible writers. The project, after being widely discussed for several years, finally took shape in England in 1870, when the Convocation of Canterbury appointed two committees to undertake the work. The ablest scholars in Hebrew and Greek literature in the country were assigned to the committees, of which one was engaged on the Old, and the other on the New Testament. They were empowered to call to their aid similar committees in America, who might work simultaneously with them. Stringent instructions were given to them to avoid making changes where they were not clearly needed for the accuracy of translation, and to preserve the idiom of the Authorized Version. Only with these safeguards and with not a little reluctance, the commission was issued. One hundred and one scholars on both sides of the Atlantic took part in the work. The committees commenced their labors early in 1871. On May 17, 1881, the Revised New Testament was issued, and on May 21, 1885, the Revised Old Testament was in the hands of the public. All that scholarship, strenuous labor and exhaustive research could do to give a faithful translation had been done within the somewhat narrow and conservative limits under which the revisers were commissioned.

## Bibles By The Million

With this improvement, there was at the same time a marked impetus in Bible circulation. The nineteenth century has been eminently a Bible-reading and a Bible-studying period. In no previous century have efforts on so gigantic a scale been made to put the Book in the hands of every one who could read it. The price was brought so low by the decrease in the cost of production, that the very poorest could possess a copy. The British and Foreign Bible Society, founded in 1804, and the American Bible Society, founded in 1816, have largely contributed to this result. Both societies were organized to issue the Bible without note or comment, and both have faithfully labored to promote its circulation. In spite of all that has been said against the Book and in spite of the fact that so large a number of persons must have been supplied, the circulation has increased from year to year. In the year ending March, 1896, the American Society alone issued 1,750,000 copies, and the British two and a half million. During its existence the American Society has sent out over sixty-one million copies and the British Society over one hundred and forty millions. The work of translation has kept pace with the demand. At the beginning of the century the Bible had been translated, in whole or in part, into thirty-eight languages. It is now translated into three hundred and eighty-one, and translators are engaged on nearly a hundred others. Nor must it be supposed that the supply was in excess of the demand. There is abundant evidence of the desire of the public to possess the Word of God. One fact alone is a conspicuous proof of this demand. In 1892 the proprietor of the *Christian Herald* of New York offered an Oxford Teacher's Bible as a premium with his journal. The offer was accepted with such avidity that edition after edition was exhausted, and it has been renewed every year since with increased demand. Through this journal alone, by this means, over three hundred and two thousand copies have been put into the hands of the people during the past five years.

With the increase in the circulation of the Word of God there has been a costly and thorough effort to gain new light on its pages. Never before have labor and money been expended so lavishly in endeavors to learn from exploration and research, historical facts which would contribute to an intelligent understanding of its history and literature. In 1865 a society called the Palestine Exploration Society was organized for the special purpose of thoroughly examining the Holy Land, investigating and identifying ancient sites and making exact maps of the country. In twenty-seven years the society, though working with the utmost economy, expended $425,000. The result of its labors has been to let a flood of light on the ancient places and the ancient customs of its people, explaining many allusions in the sacred history, poetry and prophecy that were previously dark. The Egypt Exploration Fund has also added materially to our knowledge of that country which is associated with the early history of the Chosen People. But the most valuable aid to Bible study came from the discovery of the Assyrian Royal Library, a series of clay tablets and cylinders covered with cuneiform inscriptions which were deciphered by Mr. George Smith of the British Museum. From these and from the records on the monuments of Egypt historical information has been derived of inestimable value in the study of the Bible.

## A Great Missionary Era

One of the most prominent characteristics of the Church of Christ in this century has been its phenomenal missionary activity. Its zeal in this cause, the devotion and courage of its missionaries and the amount of money expended have had no parallel in the previous history of the Church. Already a beginning had been made when the century dawned. In 1701 King William III. of England had granted a charter to the Society for the Propagation of the Gospel in Foreign Parts. In 1714 Frederick IV. of Denmark established a College of Missions and two Danish missionaries were laboring in India. In 1721 the famous Danish missionary, Hans Egede, began a work in Greenland. In 1732 the Moravian missionaries, Dober and Nitschmann, went to St. Thomas, and in the following year the Moravian Church sent missionaries to Labrador, the West Indies, South America, South Africa and India. But it was not until the last decade of the eighteenth century that the spirit which was to distinguish the next century really manifested itself. In 1792 the devotion and consecration of William Carey led to the formation of the Baptist Missionary Society, and in the following year he sailed for India as its first missionary.

In 1795 the London Missionary Society was organized, a missionary ship was purchased and the first band of missionaries sailed for the South Sea Islands. Two years later, another party sailed for South Africa, among whom were the veterans, Vanderkemp and Kitchener. Two Scottish societies were founded in 1796 and a Dutch Society in 1797. In the closing year of the century the famous Church Missionary Society was formed in the Church of England. Thus the nineteenth century opened with organizations for work in existence and pioneers few in number, but intensely in earnest in several fields of labor.

The first quarter of the century witnessed the advent of new agencies, as well as a multiplication of forces. The American Board of Commissioners for Foreign Missions was organized in 1810, the English Wesleyan Missionary Society in 1814, the American Baptist in 1814, the American Methodist in 1819, the American Protestant Episcopal in 1820, and the Berlin and Paris Missionary Societies in 1824. Thus, in the comparatively short space of thirty-two years, thirteen societies had been organized by the various denominations here and in Europe, each of which was destined to grow to proportions little contemplated by their founders. Since that time the great China Inland Mission and other undenominational societies have been founded and are sending out men and women in large numbers to the heathen world. Besides these, there have been societies of special workers which have done valuable service in aiding the missionary societies, such as the medical missionaries, the Zenana Missionaries and the university and students' volunteer movements. Statistics recently compiled show that the number of central stations in heathen lands occupied by Protestant missionaries in 1896 was 5055, with out-stations to the number of 17,813. There are now thirty-seven missionary societies in this country alone which have sent out 3512 missionaries. A library of volumes would be needed to give even a sketch of the results of the labors of these devoted men and women. The Church holds their names in holy reverence. Many of them have attained the crown of martyrdom, and a still greater number have fallen victims to the severities of uncongenial climates. Every heathen land has now associated with it the name of valiant soldiers of the Cross, who have given their lives to add it to their Master's, kingdom. In India among many others, there have been Carey, Duff, Martyn, Marshman and Ward. In China, Morrison, Milne, Taylor, John Talmage and Griffith John. In Africa, Moffat, Livingstone, Hannington and Vanderkemp. In the South Seas, Williams, Logan and Paton, while Judson of Burmah and a host of noble men and women in every clime, have toiled and suffered, not counting their lives dear unto them, that they might preach to the heathen the unsearchable riches of Christ.

## Preaching To Heathen At Home

The zeal for the propagation of the Gospel among the heathen, has been paralleled by the efforts put forth for the evangelization of the people in nominally Christian lands. In this enterprise the front rank on both sides of the Atlantic has been occupied by the Methodist Church. Its system of itinerary, relieving its ministers in part from exhausting study, and so giving them time and opportunity for pastoral work and aggressive evangelistic effort, its welcome of lay assistance in pulpit service and its system of drill and inspection in the class-meeting, have all combined to develop its working resources and increase its aggressive power. The fact that there are now in the world over thirty million Methodists of various kinds, makes it difficult to realize that when the century began, John Wesley had been dead only nine years. This century consequently has witnessed the growth and development of that mighty organization from the seed sown by that one consecrated man and his helpers. It is doubtful whether in politics or society there is any fact of the century so remarkable as this. The Church Wesley founded has split into sections in this land and in England, but the divisions are one at heart, and the name of Methodist is the common precious possession of them all. A great writer has contended with much force that the world at this day knows no such unifier of nationalities and societies as the Methodist Church. When the young man leaves the parental roof of a Methodist family for some distant city, or some foreign land, the pangs of anxiety are alleviated by the knowledge that wherever he may be, there will be some Methodist Church where he will find friends, and some Methodist class-leader who will look after his most important interests. The magnificent Methodist organization, unequalled outside the Roman Catholic Church, has developed within the century, and its aggressive forces have been felt throughout Christendom. All the denominations have received an impetus from its abundant energy and each in its measure has caught the contagion of its activities. In country districts, in the great cities and in foreign lands, its representatives, loyal to their Church and the principles of its founder, are pressing forward in self-denial and apostolic fervor foremost everywhere in the van of the Christian army.

Kindred with the Methodist in its enthusiasm and still more highly organized, is the youngest of all the religious organizations—the Salvation Army. In its origin, a daughter of the Methodist Church, with a strong resemblance in spirit and purpose and methods to its mother, the Salvation Army has a mission peculiarly its own. It too has grown with a rapidity unexampled in the religious history of other centuries. More than one quarter of the century had passed when William Booth first saw the light, more than half the century had passed before he had begun to give his life to his Master's service. From 1857 to 1859 he was simply a Methodist minister, at an unimportant town, appointed by his conference, sparsely paid, and certain to be removed to another sphere at the end of his term. In 1865, he and his devoted wife resigned home and income and dependence on conference for support, and went to London. They settled in the poorest and most degraded district of the city, and began to preach in tents, in cellars, in deserted saloons, under railroad arches, in factories and in any place which could be had for nothing, or at a low rental. The people gathered in multitudes wherever Mr. Booth and his wife preached, veritable heathen, many of them, who knew nothing of the Bible and had never attended a religious service in their lives. Converts were numerous and they were required to testify to the change in their souls and their lives and to become missionaries in their turn. In 1870 an old market was purchased in the densest centre of poverty in London and was made the headquarters of the Mission. Bands of men and women were sent out to hold meetings, sing hymns and "give their testimony" in the open-air, in saloons, or any resort where an audience could be gathered. These bands were busy every night in a hundred wretched districts of the great city, and at every stand, some poor forlorn creatures would be gathered in and encouraged to begin a new life in faith in Christ. Some method of organization became necessary, and was eventually devised. The perfect obedience and confidence manifested everywhere to the man who directed the movement, and the entire dependence of every worker on him for guidance and support, may have suggested the military system. However that may be, the military organization was adopted, and a perfect system framed with the aid of Railton Smith, and a few other clever organizers who were attracted to Mr. Booth's side by the novelty of his methods, and his marvelous success. In the spring of 1878, the plans were all matured and the new movement became a compact and powerful religious force. Since that time it has spread throughout England, into several European lands, to the United

States, and Canada, to India, Australia and South Africa. Its autocratic character has been steadfastly maintained. General Booth has retained absolute control of every officer in his service and has the management of the enormous income of the army. Occasionally there has been mutiny which has been overcome by tact or prompt discipline, and not until this year (1896), when General Booth's son, Ballington, who was his representative in the United States, resigned rather than be removed from his command, has there been any formidable defiance of the supreme and despotic government of the world-wide organization. The methods of the Army are unconventional and are shocking to staid, respectable members of churches, but criticism is out of place in any method which will redeem the masses in the numbers won by the Salvation Army.

# Churches Drawing Together

A notable characteristic of the religious life of the century, especially in the latter half of it, has been a desire manifested in various quarters, and in different ways, for union among the denominations. That organic union could be attained, no practical man could hope. Uniformity could not be expected, even if it could be proved to be desirable, but friendly association was possible, and there were many who contended that there ought to be a recognition of brotherhood and comradeship, which might issue in some attempt at co-operation. This was the conviction of many prominent preachers and laymen on both sides of the Atlantic, early in the century. And truly the condition of the world and of society was of a character to force such a conviction on the minds of intelligent men. Infidelity was rampant, and intemperance, gambling, unchastity, and other forms of vice were practiced with unblushing effrontery. On the other side, the churches, which should have been waging war on all ungodliness, were fighting each other, contending about the questions on which they differed, and exhausting their strength in internecine conflict. Was it not time, men were asking, that the forces that were on the side of godliness united in opposition to evil? After long discussion, and some opposition, this feeling took practical shape in the Evangelical Alliance. At a meeting held in London in 1846 eight hundred representatives of fifty denominations were assembled. It was found that however widely they differed on questions of doctrine and church government, there was practical agreement on a large number of vital subjects, such as the need of religious education, the observance of the Lord's Day, and the evil influence of infidelity. An organization was effected, on the principles of federation, to secure united action on subjects on which all were agreed, and this organization has been maintained to the present time. Branches have been formed in twenty-seven different lands, each dealing with matters peculiarly affecting the community in which it operates, and by correspondence, and periodical international conferences, keeping in touch with each other. Its usefulness has been proved in the success of its efforts to secure tolerance in several lands, where men were being persecuted for conscience' sake, though much still remains to be done on this line. Perhaps the most conspicuous result of its work is the general observance throughout Christendom of the first complete week of every year as a week of prayer. The proposal for such an observance was made in 1858. Since that time the Alliance has issued every year a list of subjects which are common objects of desire to all Evangelical Christians. On each day of the week, prayer is now offered in every land for the special blessing which is suggested as the topic for the day.

From the same spirit of Christian brotherhood which took shape in the Evangelical Alliance, came at later dates other movements which are yet in their infancy. One of these is the Reunion Conference which meets annually at Grindelwald in Switzerland. Its object is to find a basis for organic union of the Protestant Episcopal Church with Congregationalists, Presbyterians, Methodists and other evangelical denominations. The meetings have been hitherto remarkably harmonious, and suggestions of mutual concessions have been made which have been favorably considered. A less ambitious, and therefore more hopeful movement of like spirit, is that of the Municipal or Civic Church. Its aim is the organization of a federative council of the churches of a city, or of sections of a city, for united effort in social reform, benevolent enterprise and Christian government. It proposes to substitute local co-operation for the existing union on denominational lines, or to add the one to the other. It would unite the Methodist, Baptist, Congregational and other churches in a city, or district, in a movement to restrict the increase of saloons, to insist on the enforcement of laws against immorality and to promote the moral and spiritual welfare of the community. The united voice of the Christians of a city uttered by a council, in which all are represented, would unquestionably exercise an influence more potent than is now exerted by separate action. To these movements must be added another which has been launched under the name of the Brotherhood of Christian Unity. This is a fraternity of members of churches and members of no church, who yet accept Christ as their leader and obey the two cardinal precepts of Christianity—love to God and love to man. Its object is to promote brotherly feeling among Christians and a sense of comradeship among men of different creeds. All these movements are an indication of the spirit of the time. As one of the leaders has said, their aim is not so much to remove the fences which divide the denominations, as to lower them sufficiently to enable those who are within them to shake hands over them. In no previous century since the disintegrating tendency began to manifest itself, has this spirit of brotherly recognition of essential unity been so general, or has taken a shape so hopeful of practical beneficence.

## Organized Activities

Effective influence to the same end has been set in motion, incidentally, by an organization which was originated for a different purpose. This is the Christian Endeavor Society, which is one of the latest of the important religious movements of the century. It was primarily designed to promote spiritual development among young people. It had its birth in 1881 in a Congregational Church at Portland, Me. Dr. Francis E. Clark, the pastor of the church, had a number of young people around him who had recently made public profession of faith in Christ and pledged themselves to His service. Precisely what that implied, may not have been definitely understood by any of them. As every pastor is aware, the period immediately following such a profession is a critical time in the life of every young convert. In the college or the office, or the store, the youth comes in contact with people who have made no profession of the kind, and he is apt to ask himself, and to be asked, in what way he differs from them. The early enthusiasm of his new relation to the Church is liable to decline, and he may become doubtful whether any radical change has taken place in him. He does not realize that he is at the beginning of a period of growth, a gradual process, which is to be lifelong. Taking his conception of personal religion from the sermons he has heard and the appeals that have been made to him, he has a tendency to regard conversion as an experience complete and final, an occult mysterious transformation, effected in a moment and concluded. Disappointment is inevitable, and when non-Christian influences are Strong, there is a probability of his drifting into indifference. Dr. Clark was aware of this fact, as other pastors were, by sad experience, and he sought means to remedy it. Some plan was needed which would help the young convert and teach him how to apply his religion to his daily life, to make it an active influence, instead of a past experience. The plan Dr. Clark adopted was of an association of young people in his Church, who should meet weekly for prayer and mutual encouragement and helpfulness, with so much of an aggressive quality as to exert an influence over young people outside its membership. The plan succeeded. The religious force in the soul, so liable to become latent, became active, and the young converts made rapid progress. Dr. Clark explained his experiment to other pastors, who tried it with like results. The remedy for a widespread defect was found. It was adopted on all hands and by all evangelical denominations. It spread from church to church, from town to town and into foreign lands. Annual conventions of these Christian Endeavor Societies were held, at which forty or fifty thousand young people, representing societies in all sections of the country with an aggregate membership of about two million souls, were present to recount their experience and pledge themselves anew to the service. The basis of their association was made so broad that Christians of every denomination could heartily unite in its profession of faith. Thus, in addition to the primary design, a basis of Christian inter-denominational union was incidentally discovered, and the Methodist and the Presbyterian, the Congregationalist and Episcopalian found themselves united in a common bond for a common purpose. The movement in these present years shows no signs of decrease, but is still growing in numbers, power and influence, and promises to be one of the most potent factors of religious life which springing up in this century will go on to influence the next.

The idea of association and combination in religious life, of which Christian Endeavor is the most extensive illustration, has been embodied during the century in other forms. Springing directly from the Christian Endeavor Society, are the Epworth League in the Methodist Church, and the Baptist Young People's Union in the Baptist communion. The two organizations are practically identical in principle and purpose with the Christian Endeavor Society and differ from it only in the absence of the inter-denominational character. The heads of the Methodist Church apprehended danger to their young people in their being members of a society not under direct Methodist control and feared that they might eventually be lost to Methodism. The Baptists, on the other hand, were not concerned on the question of control, but feared that the association of their young people with the young people of other churches might lead them to think lightly of the peculiar rite which separates them from other denominations, and to diminish its importance in their esteem. Both denominations therefore organized societies of the same kind, to keep their young people within the denominational fold.

Another organization which has attained large membership and has become international, is that of the King's Daughters. As its name indicates, it was primarily intended for women, though as it extended, it added as an adjunct a membership for men as King's Sons. It also was inter-denominational in character, and its objects were more directly identified with the philanthropic side of the religious life than were those of the societies previously mentioned. It originated in a meeting of ten ladies, held in New York, in 1886, at which plans were discussed for aiding the poor, the unfortunate and the distressed in mind, body or soul. They were all Christian ladies who recognized the duty of ministering in Christ's name to those who were in need and so fulfilling His injunction of kindly service. The plan finally adopted was to organize circles of ten members each, who should be pledged to use their opportunities, as far as they were able, for Christian ministration. Each member agreed to wear, as a badge of the

Order, a small silver Maltese Cross, bearing the initials, I.H.N., representing the motto, "In His Name." Every circle was to be left free to apply the principle of service as it saw fit, or as special circumstances might suggest, and all the circles to be under the direction and limited control of a central council. The plan, subsequently modified as experience suggested, was widely adopted. The circles have worked in a variety of ways, visiting hospitals and prisons, making garments for the poor, raising funds for the needy, aiding the churches and rendering service in various ways in which kindly Christian women are so effective.

Still another form of combination in Christian work has distinguished this century. In 1844 George Williams, a London dry goods merchant employing a large number of young men, made an effort to provide them with a species of Christian club. His own experience as a young man fresh from a country home, suddenly inducted into the temptations of city life, suggested to him the kind of help such young men needed. A Christian friend in a great city to help a new-comer, to find him wholesome amusement in the evenings, and to put him on his guard against the pitfalls that were set for his unwary feet, might, Mr. Williams was convinced, save many a young man from ruin. To provide them with such friends and to furnish a place of meeting for reading, converse and amusement, was the problem the kindly Christian man attempted to solve. Out of his effort grew the institution we know as the Young Men's Christian Association, which has its mission in nearly every large town in this country and in England. The young man of this century can go into no considerable town without finding a commodious hall, with well-equipped library and reading-room, generally with a gymnasium attached, and with a host of young men ready to make his acquaintance and surround him with Christian influences. In many towns, the institution has developed from the purely religious enterprise into a many-sided effort to give practical educational training and to attract young men to it by the help it renders them in secular pursuits. The institution as it now exists, must be counted as one of the most beneficent in its far-reaching influence that the century has produced.

# Humanitarian Work

Kindred in spirit, but differing essentially in operation, is the institution, peculiarly a product of nineteenth century religion, which we know as the Social or College Settlement. Though it does not claim a distinctively religious character, its principles are so thoroughly identical with Christianity, that no survey of the religious life of the century would be complete without a recognition of it. It is the spirit that brought the Founder of Christianity to the earth, to live a lowly life among men, which inspires the Social Settlement. It is generally an unostentatious house in some crowded neighborhood, where the people are poor and life is hard. In the house are a number of college-bred men, or women, who come in relays and live there for a week or a month or longer. They do no missionary work, do not preach, or denounce, or instruct their neighbors, but they live among them a cleanly, helpful, friendly life, welcoming them cordially as visitors, advising them if advice is sought, rendering help in difficulties and being neighborly in the best sense of the word. There are concerts in the house, exhibitions of pictures, children's parties and amusements of various kinds to which all the neighbors are welcome. Charity is no part of the Settlement's programme. It does not give, but it extends a brotherly hand, and in a spirit of friendship and equality seeks to do a brother's part in brightening lowly lives. Hundreds of such institutions are in operation on both sides the Atlantic. To the credit of this century be it said that it has seen in these institutions the Parable of the Good Samaritan made a living fact in intelligent organization.

Tending directly toward the same object, is the religious enterprise now commonly known as the Institutional Church. It is a distinct gain to the church if the people in its vicinity discover that it is anxious to help them to a better and happier life in this world, as well as guiding them to happiness in the next. The Divine Founder of Christianity never ignored the fact that men have bodies which need saving, as well as souls, and some of His followers are following His example. Their churches do not stand closed and silent from Sunday to Sunday, but are open every day and evening, busy with some form of practical helpfulness. Temperance societies, coal clubs, sewing meetings, dime savings banks, gymnasiums, boys' clubs, and a host of helpful associations tending to the betterment of life, find their home under the roof of the church, and the pastor and his helpers are finding out the social and economical needs of the people by actual contact with them and devising means to supply them. The critics say this is not the business of the church, but they are not found among the people who derive benefit from this form of thoughtful interest in their welfare.

## The Sunday School

Of all the products of this prolific nineteenth century, the one most extensive and most profitable to the church still remains to be mentioned. Though this century did not see the birth of the Sunday School, it has witnessed its wonderful development. In June, 1784, Robert Raikes published his famous letter outlining his plan for the religious instruction of children on the Lord's Day, and before the close of the year, John Wesley wrote that he found Sunday Schools springing up wherever he went, and added with prophetic insight: "Perhaps God may have a deeper end therein than men are aware of. Who knows but some of these schools may become nurseries for Christians?" Within five years, a quarter of a million children were gathered into the Sunday Schools. So much had already been done before the beginning of the century. But even then men did not realize whereunto the movement was destined to grow. Probably no enterprise has really exerted a deeper and stronger influence on the religious life of the time. Children have entered the schools, passed through their grades, have become teachers in their turn, and their descendants have followed in their footsteps, until now we can scarcely bring ourselves to believe that a little more than a hundred years ago the Sunday School was unknown. The organization of Sunday School Unions, the introduction of the International Lesson System, and the City, State and National Conventions are all the developments of this century. The thought that a million and a half of Sunday School teachers are now engaged in every clime, Sunday by Sunday, in teaching the children and young people the truths of Christianity is enough to fill the mind of the Christian with thankfulness and hope.

# Pulpit And Press

It would be beyond the scope of an article of this character to attempt to recall the names of the eminent preachers of the century. It has been singularly rich in men of eloquence, depth of thought and high culture. A few, however, are distinguished among the noble army by the phenomenal character of their work. Of these probably no name is so widely known as that of Rev. T. DeWitt Talmage, D.D. One of the most remarkable phenomena of the religious world in this century, is the fact that every week one preacher should address an audience numbered by millions. The fact is unprecedented. Of all classes of readers, the number of those who read sermons is considered the smallest, yet this century has produced a preacher whose sermons command a public larger than that of a fascinating novelist. For thirty years the newspapers have been publishing Dr. Talmage's sermons in every city of his own land, in every English-speaking land and in many foreign lands where they are translated for publication. It is a significant fact, which should gratify every Christian, that the man whose words reach regularly and surely the largest audience in the world should be a preacher of the Gospel.

To no man in any walk of life, whether politician, editor or author, has the opportunity of impressing his thoughts on his generation that Dr. Talmage enjoys been given in such fulness. Next in extent of influence, and with a like faculty of reaching immense and widely scattered masses of people, was the late Charles Haddon Spurgeon, a preacher of singularly homely power, Calvinistic in theology, epigrammatic in style, and with an earnest evangelical spirit which had a powerful influence on both hearers and readers. His sermons, like those of Dr. Talmage, were read in every land and were instrumental in conversions wherever they went. Strongly resembling Mr. Spurgeon in his strong evangelicalism, as well as in homely eloquence, is Mr. D.L. Moody. During this century probably no man has addressed so large a number of people. In this country and in England such audiences have thronged the buildings in which he preached as no other orator has ever addressed on religious subjects, and the influence of his words is demonstrated by the thousands who through his appeals have been led to Christ.

We are nearing the end of the century. Looking back over the events in the religious world which have marked its history, one characteristic is prominent above all others. It is the operation of the force to which an eminent writer has given the name of "spiritual dynamics." The world does not need a dogma, or a creed, so much as it needs power. It needs power to live right, to do right, to love God and man, to pity the fallen, to relieve the needy, the power of being good, of leading a spiritual life. This power it finds in Christ and the whole tendency of the religious life of the century is to get back to him. Conduct rather than creed, love rather than theology, have been the watchwords of the church. The spirit of Christ, His teachings, His character, His example, are the centre of attraction which holds His church together and endues it with the power which shall yet subdue the world.

CPSIA information can be obtained
at www.ICGtesting.com
Printed in the USA
LVHW041006020323
740706LV00008B/879

9 789356 906037